"Bryan Citrin is an influencer, an idea generator and a resource for a generation. *Wild Expectance* is a tool to inspire and equip you to step up and upgrade from mere existence to the life you were created to live. In this book, you will find principles, stories and concepts that will cause you to tap into something greater that is awaiting you. Read this book and start your journey!"

— **SEAN SMITH**
Author of Prophetic Evangelism
Speaker, Podcaster, & Father
SeanAndChristaSmith.com

"With real-life examples, clear teaching from Scripture, and easy to understand explanations, Bryan clarifies what it practically looks like to step out in faith and boldly follow God. This book has the power to activate you into your destiny. I encourage you to read every word, adjust your expectancy to match God's word, then boldly engage in your own adventure with God!"

— **CALEB BROWN**
President of Ministry Training Network
CEO of Venatrust

"Bryan Citrin will always be one of my favorite people. I can attest to the many crazy stories of Bryan's life. I have met many authors and few of them really live out what they write. I have watched Bryan live this life over the last two decades. Bryan is both a business genius, a world-class leader, and also a man of deep faith. When dark storm clouds moved in and it started raining shortly before my wedding, I sought out Bryan to pray. And we all watched his faith change the weather. This book will change the way you think about both business and faith, in a really good way. I honestly can't think of anyone that shouldn't go on this wild journey."

— **JOE BAKER**
Founder of Save the Storks
CEO of Adventure Homes & Superhero Sidekick

"Scripture tells us that God is forming us even while we are in our mother's womb and that He has His plan and purpose in mind as He does. Bryan does a great job encouraging you to embrace God's design for your life as nothing in life can be more fulfilling. As our life embraces God's design we can embrace *Wild Expectance*."

— **STEVE GREEN**
President of Hobby Lobby
Chairman of the board, Museum of the Bible

"The words 'wild' and 'expectance' are more than just ink on paper when it comes to Bryan Citrin. His ability to live out his faith in radical ways has inspired me to consider how I can live out my wildest God-given dreams in the face of doubt. If you take the time to read this book, and you should, I believe his story will inspire you to do the same."

— **MATT HAMMITT**
2x Grammy Nominated Artist
3x Dove Award-Winning Songwriter
Author & Speaker

"Bryan is passionate about the things of God and fearlessly lives out this desire to draw people closer to God. He seeks out God-opportunities to touch lives, whether it's sitting in his car at a red light or traveling to a foreign country. From Haiti to the campus of UCLA, I've seen him live out his conviction not just with words but with actions. This book will help you live boldly and look for divine setups in your daily life."

— **ELISHA CHAN**
Executive Director of Fair Trade LA
Founder of Impactful Missions
ImpactfulMissions.org

"Bryan is a prime example of boldness and the confidence we can have in God to change lives. His life demonstrates that we can be used by God in the wildest ways when we have an expectation on Him. The principles and anecdotes in this book will inspire anyone who wants to partner with God and make a greater impact in this world."

— **NATHAN FRANCIS, PHD**
Research Scientist, UCLA

"Bryan's desire to chase after Jesus has led him through some incredible faith adventures. This book and the stories interwoven within will not only elevate your faith, but encourage you to live out your walk with Jesus boldly and with confidence because you know a great adventure awaits ahead. *Wild Expectance* will inspire you to start asking the Lord where He wants to stretch and deepen your faith, so you can live a life of greater Kingdom impact."

— **ALISSA CIRCLE**
Author & Speaker
Founder & CEO of Pollinate Media Group

"Few are impacting the spheres of business and ministry like Bryan Citrin. His faith is contagious and his practical application is empowering. *Wild Expectance* is a book that will inspire and instruct you to soar higher."

— MARK FRANCEY
Pastor of Oceans Church
OceansChurch.com

WILD
EXPECTANCE
START LIVING YOUR LIFE HOW GOD DESIGNED IT

BRYAN CITRIN

Published by NEWTYPE
1805 Hilltop Drive
Suite 211
Redding, CA 96002

wildexpectance.com
info@wildexpectance.com

Editing Team: Dr. Gerald C. Simmons, Dr. Erin Almond, Tiara Brown, and Rainah Davis.

ISBN: 978-1-952421-27-3
Library of Congress Control Number: 2022907188
Printed in the United States of America

Individuals, churches, and business groups may order books from Bryan Citrin directly, or from the publisher. Retailers and wholesalers should order from our distributors. Bryan Citrin is available to speak for your church, business, or conference event on a variety of topics. Visit WildExpectance.com/Invite for booking information.

DEDICATION

In honor of my mother, Joan. Through many trials and tribulations, she did her best to raise me and my brother, David, with the truth of Jesus despite my father's resistance—a nonreligious Jewish man. I'm grateful my father eventually accepted Jesus Christ as his Lord and Savior on Rosh Hashanah, the Jewish New Year, about five years before writing this.

In memory of my father, who passed away just a few weeks after I began writing this book. Despite practical and emotional difficulties, I pressed on with my writing. My prayer is that my father's legacy will live on through the positive ripple effect into eternity this book will produce for millions worldwide.

TABLE OF CONTENTS

FOREWORD

It was a serendipitous moment when Bryan Citrin and I shared the stage together for the first time. He had just been featured as the marketing authority in the current edition of *Chiropractic Economics*, a leading chiropractic magazine mailed to countless chiropractors across the United States. The publication date aligned perfectly with my Christ-Centered Chiropractic conference, where we equipped and empowered top doctors from around the nation to reach the masses. As you read this book, you'll soon discover that Bryan's commitment to God and His people has given him great favor to accomplish His purposes.

It might impress you to know that after he spoke, instead of jumping on a flight back to his home in Los Angeles to focus on his business, Bryan boarded a plane for Vietnam for his fifth mission trip to that nation in a single year.

I have been fortunate to write over 20 books and blessed enough to see two of them reach *The New York Times* best sellers list. My church curriculum has been translated into dozens of languages through my work with the Global Church initiative, I have been the editor for two devotional Bibles, and my programs have been used by tens of thousands of corporations, churches, schools, and sports teams in countries all over the globe. I've worked with some of the world's most influential pastors, have opened over 150 chiropractic clinics, and have grown numerous companies to millions in just their first twelve months in operation. Yet, it is God that has given me the power to do it all, and I know He is responsible for it all. I believe if you let God fully use you, there is more for you in this life than you think there is right now.

When working to achieve success, I am always careful to look for experts in key areas where I am not an expert. Nearly every business endeavor requires online marketing, and Bryan is who I turn to for expert advice in this field. As important as it is to work with the best, it is even more vital that those people love Jesus. Bryan is not only a voice for digital knowledge; he is a voice for Christ. Expertise plus the will of God is the equation for supernatural growth. Smart, hard-working people can seem to succeed without God, but only *this* formula will allow you to experience a life of *wild expectance*.

Jesus does not say that a journey with Him is free of trouble. In fact, He says the opposite, "In this world, you will have trouble" (John 16:33). While He did not promise life would be easy, Jesus does promise He will always be with you. That is what I love and appreciate about Bryan's success that he has graciously shared here. He takes you on a behind-the-scenes journey from college, through his missionary work, and to his thriving career and committed service to Christ through all of the ups, downs, and wild adventures of faith. These stories will give you principles that will take both your spiritual and entrepreneurial life to the next level and act like a roadmap towards your destiny.

No one has to settle for a life of mediocrity. I encourage everyone I meet to discover God's purpose for their lives, reach their potential, and complete God's assignment for their life. If God has called you to win your race, God forbid you do not win your race.

I spent many years as a doctor for some of the U.S. Olympic Teams. At the 2012 Olympics in London, I was deeply moved by their theme for those games: "Amazing awaits!" God tells us the same thing. He declares to us all that He has zero plans to harm us but rather to prosper us, give us hope and a future (Jeremiah 29:11). In fact, "We know that in all things God works for the good of those who love Him, who have been called according to His purpose" (Romans 8:28). Everything you have been through, are going to go through, and all that you currently are experiencing, is God mapping out a plan for your best life. All you need to do is take the next step.

FOREWORD

This book is a great start. Read it, apply it, and be empowered by the Holy Spirit through its truths and meanings. *Wild Expectance* is a gift from God that everyone has the opportunity to experience.

Amazing awaits!

—DR. BEN LERNER
2x *New York Times* Best Selling Author
CEO & Founder of The Ultimate Influence Group

EXPERIENCE THE BOOK

A book will only help you if you read it, retain it, and apply it. Because of this, I have created a free interactive experience while you read to make this book more memorable and enhance your book reading experience. This will get you access to free corresponding bonus content, videos, and some fun surprises along the way. To get the full experience, be sure to register now before you read any further at www.WildExpectance.com/ExperienceTheBook

CHAPTER 01

ANSWERING THE CALL

I never wanted to be a missionary. It was my desire to make a lot of money and fund the Gospel. I was about to graduate from Missouri State University with my Bachelor of Science degree in Entrepreneurship. You do not need a college degree in this to launch a business, but it sounded "cool." Therefore, I studied hard, earned good grades, was elected president of the Entrepreneurship Association, and I wrote an eighty-five-page business plan with my friend (who agreed that this seemed more like a doctoral thesis). It was now time for me to launch out and start my million-dollar business empire.

Then, everything unexpectedly changed. I recently started attending a new church, and as I was praying during worship, I sensed God was speaking to me. It wasn't an audible sound, not a booming voice from Heaven, but a soft thought that wouldn't go away. It made no sense! After the service, I called my brother and told him the problem: I told him that I sensed God wanted me to move out to Los Angeles, one of the most expensive cities in the world, and work for *free*! "If you think God is calling you to do that, then you need to call Winston," my brother reassured me.

Winston Bui was my brother's mentor and the Chi Alpha pastor at the University of Missouri. A few years before I graduated college, Winston felt called to transition from Missouri. Being obedient to God's leading, he led a team out to Los Angeles to pioneer a Chi Alpha chapter at the University of

California: Los Angeles (UCLA). Winston had a powerful story, having come to America as a child from Vietnam. Winston and his family were refugees from the Vietnam War and escaped on a boat around the Fall of Saigon. Although raised Buddhist, while he was in high school, he became a Christian after his friend invited him to a youth service at a local church. During his college days, Winston felt called to become a campus pastor and a missionary to college students.

"It was on the bottom of my list to move out to Los Angeles and work with you," I told Winston in person (some months later, after my decision to move to Los Angeles was official). "Bryan, you weren't even on my list," he retorted. "We haven't taken on a new intern in a year and a half, and we've turned down everyone who asked. I was driving on the 405 highway, about to go on a week-long fast, when the Spirit of God spoke to me. He told me I was going to receive an unexpected phone call very soon, and my answer better be 'Yes.' And Bryan, you called me within minutes."

THERE IS A TREASURE TROVE OF RICH EXPERIENCES GOD HAS PREPARED FOR US BEFORE THE FOUNDATIONS OF THE WORLD IF WE WILL STOP, LISTEN, AND ACT ON WHAT HE WANTS TO SAY TO US.

Little did I know that this God-directed conversation would result in Winston becoming an important mentor of mine. His confirmation brought me great encouragement as I prepared to make one of the biggest decisions of my life. Perhaps you can relate to my testimony or relief in knowing that I wasn't making a grave mistake.

As humans, sometimes we become so consumed by negative news, the fear of the unknown, and the desire for safety that we miss out on incredible opportunities and adventures to live a life of purpose and fulfillment. I believe that God has an exciting journey prepared for each of us to discover, and I am sure that I am not the only one who has imagined a perfect life five, ten, or even twenty years from now. I bet we have all dreamed of the house that we will live in, the career path we will take, who our spouse will be, who our children will become, and so forth. But if we are not continually looking to God to help guide us in this process, I believe we are missing out on incredible moments and memories that could affect us and countless others for generations.

There is a treasure trove of rich experiences God has prepared for us before the foundations of the world if we will stop, listen, and act on what He wants to say to us. His leadership won't always be safe, easy, or fun, but I believe that the experiences will be worth it in the end. I believe that God wants to speak to us and guide us through life's easy and difficult situations if we let Him. Perhaps you have had that feeling of trusting your gut against all logic? What do you think God is currently speaking to you?

In this book, I will show you how being consistently led by God and doing what He says will lead to incredible opportunities and adventures; it will also impact your life in ways that you never imagined to be possible.

God is the most creative being in existence. He knows everything about everything, and He has prepared an incredible journey for you here on the earth if you will only let Him guide you. Winston told me that I wasn't thinking big enough if I could achieve my dreams on my own. God needs big thinkers who He can give ideas to who have the audacity to believe that they can make a global impact as they execute God's plans.

For example, for as long as I can remember, my brother wanted to be a fighter pilot. He would often play flight simulator computer games. He had a replica joystick of a F-16 for a controller. He was obsessed with model planes. Eventually, he went through Air Force ROTC and could name any military aircraft just by its tail.

During my brother's senior year of college, he was dealt the biggest blow of his life when he did not receive a pilot slot in the military. At first, he was very angry, but learned that he had made becoming a pilot an idol before God. He had recently rededicated his life to Christ after a friend had invited him to Chi Alpha, a ministry on his campus. Through prayer and fasting, he sensed that God was leading him down a different career path. Once he firmly became set on what was the direction of the Lord, the impossible happened: he was offered his lifelong dream of becoming an Air Force pilot.

By this time, he knew that God was shifting him in a new direction, so he turned down the opportunity. After his five years of Air Force service, he departed to help do ministry with me. Then an opportunity to fulfill his desire of working overseas as a defense contractor arose, thus giving him the financial stability to significantly fund the Gospel and the flexibility to travel the world doing missions without bearing the burden of the rigorous schedule of a military pilot. His testimony is a great example of how God makes things work together for our long-term benefit when we seek God, especially for direction in important life decisions.

Over the course of my life, I have had the opportunity to travel the world with my brother and others as a full-time missionary. It wasn't always easy, and there were many times when I remember seeing more "month than money." As a result, I had to learn to listen to God and do what He said if I was going to survive being "jobless" in Los Angeles while pursuing a career as a donor-backed campus missionary. As of this writing, I have had the honor of doing missions in Haiti (twenty-eight times), Vietnam (six times), traveling throughout Europe raising money for Haiti, and even meeting with ministry alumni in China. I have toured Christian rock festivals, rock-climbed throughout the United States, attended VIP parties at the American Music Awards, and mentored some of the most influential students in the world at the University of California: Los Angeles (UCLA) and the University of Southern California (USC). This includes university professors from other nations and even a student who went on to win a gold record from RCA (An American record label owned by Sony Music Entertainment), selling over 500,000 records. At the leading of the Lord and His timing, I was able to transition back into business, become a writer on Forbes.com and even win one of the most coveted marketing awards in the world: the *2 Comma Club Award* for having made over one million dollars online through a marketing sales funnel. I accomplished all of these achievements while being led by God and living a missions-first lifestyle.

I have had the opportunity to learn from some of the most prophetic and Spirit-led leaders of our generation. I have served other missionaries, evangelists, and teachers who have impacted millions for Christ and have been able to glean their secrets for better intimacy with God. Everyone who has practiced the principles and concepts I have lived out has made a bigger impact on the world, lived a life of greater fulfillment, and, thankfully, a life filled with vibrant adventure and excitement. We are not called to live a monotonous, boring life of clocking in and out for forty years in order to truly start living.

Therefore, I want to encourage you to continue reading this book if you want to be inspired by the possibilities of what could be for your future. I am not promising that you will be rich if you read this book and follow God, but I am promising that you will live a more fulfilled life full of rich experiences and relationships. Whether you have no faith background, are a new believer in Jesus, or are a lifelong follower, whether you are young or old, it is never too late to step out into the unknown with God. He still has powerful plans prepared for you if you take the time to listen as He speaks. This book will elevate your faith to ideas you have never imagined and enable you to hear from God for yourself. I once heard it said that God gives you at least four ideas a year and that if you were to act on them, they would change your life forever—I believe that reading this book is one of those ideas you should act on now.

I ONCE HEARD IT SAID THAT GOD GIVES YOU AT LEAST FOUR IDEAS A YEAR AND THAT IF YOU WERE TO ACT ON THEM, THEY WOULD CHANGE YOUR LIFE FOREVER—I BELIEVE THAT READING THIS BOOK IS ONE OF THOSE IDEAS YOU SHOULD ACT ON NOW.

Be sure to read this book in its entirety. Each chapter is power-packed with inspirational stories and practical applications.

Whether you realize it or not, God is speaking to you every day in a variety of ways. It is important that you understand and learn His forms of communication so that you can elevate your vision and reach incredible accomplishments for His Kingdom (some you may have never thought possible). The storms of life will come, but by understanding His voice, you will learn that He will never leave you in a situation from which He will not get you out. Others are watching you, and so it is very important to set a Godly example. Become the person that you are called to be and thereby be the good influence that this generation so desperately needs.

CHAPTER 02

A LIFE WORTH LIVING

"You can't fly; you're a chicken," the Vietnamese interpreter said in English, translating the sermon of the visiting guest pastor from Vietnam. He was telling a story about a farmer, who had found an eagle egg that had rolled out of its mother's nest. Showing compassion for the egg, the farmer took it back to his farm and placed it in his roost among the chicken eggs. As time progressed, the baby eagle grew up among the chicks, but it couldn't stop thinking about what flying was like. He would daydream about flying every day after coming down off his perch on top of their coop, and he would tell his fellow chicks about it. Whenever he would bring his dreams up, his siblings would tease him. They would tell him that he was a chicken and that chickens couldn't fly.

His adoptive mother further told him that chickens were meant to stay on the ground and that it was dangerous to even think about flying. As the eagle grew older, his dreams of flying grew fainter and fainter. He continued to think and act more and more like a chicken every day. Eventually, he forgot about his dream of flying altogether. Then one afternoon, the eagle died.

I heard this story firsthand in a sermon from a Vietnamese pastor who traveled to the United States to challenge Vietnamese American pastors. "If we listen to chickens, we will eventually die like a chicken," he taught. I am firmly convinced that God is continually speaking to us about our identity and purpose. If you already know what you should do in life, do not let the pressures of society, your friends, or your family prevent you from living out your true destiny.

Through Scripture, we read how God challenges us to do the unconventional and even the impossible, but practically, what does that look like? How do we discern the voice of God in an actionable way, especially when it is easier to play it safe and blend in with the crowd? Every day we are bombarded with negativity not just through social media and television but by our own friends, family, and coworkers. Inevitably, our life becomes a reflection of our atmosphere.

It is easy to separate the expectations God had on the early disciples from what He expects of us today. After all, they walked with Jesus, talked with Jesus, and saw His many miracles firsthand. Many believers do not believe God still does miracles. Many others doubt Jesus and the disciples ever did any of the spectacular events recorded in the Bible and don't believe we can be empowered and baptized with the Holy Spirit to do the greater works Jesus talked about in John 14:12. Considering this negative perspective, how can we expect those around us to believe that God is actually speaking to us about who we should (or shouldn't) marry, a drastic career change, business startup, or entrance into a full-time donor-backed ministry?

Many times, we do not step out at God's leading because of the lies we choose to believe. Those same lies hold back and prevent our friends, family, and neighbors from reaching their true potential as well.

Do any of these sound familiar?

- You have a fear of failure and play worst-case scenarios on repeat in your mind.
- You have insecurities from past experiences and negative words from others.
- You are not confident that you actually heard from God.
- You are afraid of the unknown and are too comfortable to risk change.
- You have expectations from friends and family and are afraid to disappoint them.

- You were completely oblivious that God even wanted to speak to you.

Football can be a dangerous sport. If you stay on the bench, it's perfectly safe, and you won't get hit. However, in doing so, you won't score a touchdown, won't protect your teammates, and will never take part in the joy of helping your team win. If you never step foot on the field, your existence on the team will be mediocre at best.

Imagine lying on your deathbed and wrestling with a life of regrets, having lived insignificantly for God. Instead of being applauded by God (Matthew 25:23), the Devil instead comes to you right before your death and says, "Well done, my good and faithful servant." In reflection of your life, you think of the different doors that you didn't walk through because of conventional wisdom. You played it safe and had your average job with your average house and your average family. Nothing really significant happened because you didn't believe that God had significance planned for you.

The miracle you could have been for others never happened because you were too afraid to pray for them. Those you were called to care for found support elsewhere because you were too greedy to help them. You missed out on those memories of God's provision and protection because you never humbled yourself to ask for His help. You never took advantage of the blessings and experiences God had prepared for you because you thought being poor was normal or even a virtue.

SCOOTER FAITH

During my second year as a missionary in Los Angeles, the Lord brought to my remembrance a ministry I used to serve while I was in college. Periodically, I would drive down from Springfield, Missouri, and volunteer for Dr. Nasir Siddiki's monthly services in Tulsa, Oklahoma. Although I had not listened to any of his teachings for a few years, I knew that his ministry had exploded and that he was on television broadcasting to millions of households around the world. I wasn't surprised at his ministry's success because he was a former Muslim businessman with a powerful story.

Years earlier, Nasir was diagnosed with the worst case of shingles ever admitted to Toronto General Hospital. He had hideous blisters across his face, a 107.6-degree temperature, and his immune system soon shut down. Bedridden, he overheard two doctors speaking amongst themselves that there was nothing more that could be done for Nasir and that he wouldn't make it through the night. Despite his success, his money and modern medicine couldn't save him. Desperate, he called out to God for help.

"God, if you're real, don't let me die," Nasir pleaded.

Nasir explained that it was Jesus, not Muhammad or Allah, who answered his prayer. In his darkest moment, Jesus showed up in his hospital room and said, "I am the God of the Christians. I am the God of Abraham, Isaac, and Jacob."

The next morning, doctors were shocked he survived the night and determined the blisters on his face had stopped growing. They released Nasir from the hospital with a bag of medication and the concerning diagnosis of continued pain and blisters. Within a few days, Nasir got on his knees and cried out to God again. This time, he accepted Jesus as his savior. A few days later, every blister and his disfigured flesh fell off his face leaving him completely healed with no scars. Soon afterward, Nasir went to Bible school and committed his life to sharing his testimony and teaching others Biblical principles of success.

I first heard his testimony when he spoke at my church at 18 years old. Years later, and now in Los Angeles, I suddenly felt prompted to visit Dr. Siddiki's website.

I was shocked to learn that he was coming to Los Angeles that weekend to conduct a conference for the Crenshaw Christian Center at the Faith-Dome, a famous 10,000-seat auditorium in Los Angeles. I did not have a car and was instead driving a little blue moped scooter that couldn't even go over forty miles an hour. I even zip-tied a plastic milk crate basket on the back so I could go shopping, but that's beside the point. It's okay to judge me for the basket; I judged myself. I didn't know if my scooter could make it across town even if I wanted to attend the service. I had every reason not to go to Dr. Siddiki's conference, with negative thoughts bombarding my mind:

"Your scooter won't make it that far!"

"It's been so long that Dr. Siddiki won't even remember you."

"It's a huge church. You will be in the very back, and you won't get to talk with him."

"Nobody cares about your ministry."

Resisting these thoughts, I made the decision to go anyway. I decided not to reveal my plans to anyone else because I didn't want to be talked out of it. When I arrived, I was graciously greeted by the ushers, who walked me to the front of the church and seated me a few seats behind Dr. Siddiki. When he stood up to preach, he looked at me almost the entire time. After the service, he asked what I was doing there and invited me to have dinner with him and some others. He proceeded to invite me to dinner each night while he was in town. He would have an evening Bible study at a restaurant where he continued to teach those closest to him. It felt like how Jesus taught his disciples in a smaller setting after he preached.

> **IN HIS DARKEST MOMENT, JESUS SHOWED UP IN HIS HOSPITAL ROOM AND SAID, "I AM THE GOD OF THE CHRISTIANS. I AM THE GOD OF ABRAHAM, ISAAC, AND JACOB."**

During those dinner sessions, I was able to personally meet Pastor Fred Price Jr., who pastored the Crenshaw Christian Center. He graciously invited me to speak for their missions service for ten minutes. When the time came for me to speak at his church, I didn't even have enough money to pay rent. The money they gave me to speak was just the amount I needed to survive another month in Los Angeles. Another person I met during that evening Bible study was a federal judge who eventually bought me my first laptop. I can vividly remember walking into an Apple store a few months later and him telling me that I could get anything I wanted. Others from that evening Bible study would go on to support my ministry in a variety of ways over the years; one of them even became a business partner of mine over a decade later.

What would have happened if I didn't recognize the voice of God when He brought Dr. Siddiki to my remembrance? What if I didn't take the leap of faith to drive my rundown scooter halfway across town on side streets to attend the church service? What if I had chosen not to attend those evening dinner Bible studies? After all, I had a great reason not to attend: it rained a couple of the nights, and I needed to wear a rain jacket and rain pants just to keep dry. Thankfully, I had both of these from my experiences rock climbing in Wyoming. Out of conviction regarding the importance of attending, I put on my rain gear, got on my little blue scooter, and drove to downtown Los Angeles every night Dr. Siddiki was in town.

Have you ever felt a deep passion inside your heart to do something, whether big or small? Perhaps it was a great desire that wouldn't go away, yet your friends and family thought it was crazy. Maybe you have abandoned those desires just to please others. It might even be your own insecurities and negative thoughts telling you that you are not good enough, that you are not worthy, or that you don't deserve the happiness that the fulfillment of this desire would bring.

DO NOT ALLOW YOUR FAILURES, WHAT PEOPLE ARE SAYING ABOUT YOU, OR YOUR INSECURITIES TO DICTATE WHAT YOU CAN RECEIVE FROM GOD AND HOW HE CAN USE YOU.

If your grand idea doesn't go against Scripture and you have peace in your heart about it, then maybe it's God speaking to you, and you should pursue it. It can be difficult to take risks when you are first learning to hear from God—it can be difficult to take risks even if you have been following the leading of God your entire life!

1 Peter 5:8-9 says, "Be sober-minded; be watchful. Your adversary, the Devil, prowls around like a roaring lion, seeking someone to devour. Resist him, firm in your faith, knowing that the same kinds of suffering are being experienced by your brotherhood throughout the world."

I want to reassure you that you are not alone. Everyone has doubts, experiences pushback, and gives in to pressure at times. We all have an invisible yet very real enemy trying to prevent us from hearing and acting on God's voice. The purpose of this book is to stimulate your faith and to provide strategies for you to hear from God and navigate the battles you face every day.

You have what it takes. You don't have to miss your breakthrough, miracle, or calling. God is speaking to you every day, and even now, as you read the words on this page. Continue to read this book with an open mind to what God wants to do in your life, both big and small. Do not allow your failures, what people are saying about you, or your insecurities to dictate what you can receive from God and how He can use you.

You might be wondering, "Am I too young to step out for God? Don't I have to finish school first, find the right spouse, or have the right job before God can use me?" The answer is, "NO!" God wants to use you and speak to you where you are today. It is not your *age*—it is your *obedience* that matters. When I was just eight years old, I remember God using me to start my first business selling polished rocks. Since then, He has continued to give me numerous business ideas, and I haven't looked back.

Maybe you are asking yourself, "Am I too old to step out and do out of the ordinary things for God? Is it too late for me and my calling?" The answer for you is also, "NO!" God wants to use each of us where we are on any given day. His mercies are new every morning, and He is always looking for people, regardless of age, to say, "YES." I believe that our calling can be like a GPS: regardless of how many exits we miss, He can always reroute us to where we need to be to best serve His purpose at any given moment.

You may wonder, "Does God really care about the little things in my life? Aren't I bothering Him when I ask Him for help with the small things?" In Matthew 7:7-8, Jesus taught, "Ask, and it will be given to you; seek, and you will find; knock, and it will be opened to you. For everyone who asks receives, and the one who seeks finds, and to the one who knocks, it will be opened." He didn't say that you should only ask if it is really, really big; God wants to be part of our daily lives and partner with us in both big and small decisions.

You may feel that you are not righteous enough to hear from God or to be used by Him. Remember that both Moses and Paul were murderers, yet God was able to use them to write significant portions of the Bible!

You are the star of your story. It is time to start living a life worth reading. 1 Corinthians 2:9 says, "...What no eye has seen, nor ear heard, nor the heart of man imagined, what God has prepared for those who love Him." God has prepared some incredible memories, adventures, blessings, and even trials, for you. It will not always be easy, but your willingness to hear from Heaven and act on it will result in fruit that will last for eternity. There is an incredible peace that comes with hearing His voice and truly knowing Him. God knows you better than you know yourself, so stop worrying about your current situation and start listening. You will be glad that you did! His vision of you is greater than you could even imagine.

CHAPTER 03

LIVING WILD EXPECTANCE

Your God-given potential is not based on your current bank account. Instead, it is based upon what God says is possible, mixed with what your faith will allow. Therefore, keep reading this book to increase your faith! Whether you're young or old, it's not too late. You can still jump into a career that excites you. It's not too late to step out and serve others, try something unique, have fun, or even do something dangerous. If you get scared, you can always step back into your comfort zone, and I bet that no one will even notice!

I've been blessed with countless stories of God's direction, provision, and creative ideas. It's not because God loves me more, but it is because I've been willing to slow down and listen. I had to learn not only how to hear God but also how to actually act on His ideas even when they seemed *wild*! It's a lifestyle I've tried to practice for as long as I can remember.

BUILDING AN EARLY FOUNDATION

Starting a Christian apparel business is not exactly what I expected to hear the Lord tell me to do as a 16-year-old while sitting in Spanish class. While other guys my age were focused on girls and drinking, I sensed I was supposed to start this business. It was a faint God-inspired thought that led me to learn graphic design, purchase blank shirts from a wholesaler, and find a local screen-printer.

I was even able to get three local stores to carry my shirts and had a booth a couple of times at Crossover, the annual Christian rock festival my city hosted. This decision as a high schooler would open doors, relationships, and opportunities that still yield dividends nearly two decades later.

In God's eyes, it was never about getting rich by selling Christian shirts. God was instead using this to build a foundation of relationships and opportunities for the future. I didn't understand this at the time, and my lack of monetary success left me with severe doubt and feelings of insignificance that followed me into college. I still remember standing at the altar during one of Dr. Siddiki's church services my sophomore year in college as I fought off insecurities.

What was I thinking, starting a Christian apparel business? I thought to myself. Unfortunately, I was inspired by the "Abreadcrumb and Fish" style of shirts that imitated Abercrombie and other popular brands. No one wanted cheesy Christian T-shirts with a picture of a floppy disk that read "Jesus Saves" or a credit card with "Discover Him, He's Everywhere You'll Ever Be." I continued thinking, *My business isn't going anywhere. Were the past three years I spent on that business a waste of time?* My thoughts went on a downward negative spiral.

It was right then that Dr. Siddiki prayed over me, a nineteen-year-old entrepreneur. I've experienced things like this before, but this was different. This man addressed exactly what I was thinking. Was it magic? How did he read my mind? There is no way he could have known those thoughts. He had a prophetic Word from God for me, and this was right out of 1 Corinthians 12:8-10, where Paul explains the gifts of the Holy Spirit. "That still happens today?" you might be asking yourself. Yes, it does still happen, and I write about this more in chapter ten.

After the service, I asked the sound team if they turned the microphone off during the prayer time. To my surprise, they hadn't. They actually had a recording of the prophetic Word that was spoken over me, which I'm about to share.

"Big ideas, big plans, they're from Me. Don't let anyone, don't let ANY-ONE pour water on you. Don't let ANYONE quench that hunger to do great things for Me, for I am raising you up, and in due season my son, you will do great exploits. I'm looking for big thinkers, and I found one right here. Don't despise that, don't despise that, don't despise small beginnings because as you start small, it will grow, and I will show you what to do and where to go (says the Spirit of God). And you will know that it is Me, for you will hear My voice, you will obey My voice and the voice of strength, and you will not fail" (Dr. Nasir Siddiki, September 2nd, 2006, Tulsa, Oklahoma).

I encourage you to read that prophetic Word again that God had for me in my moment of turmoil. This time read it as if God were speaking directly to you because He is. God needs you to think big. As you continue to read this book, I believe you will see yourself from a new lens. You will begin to see yourself as someone who can accomplish great things for His glory. You will see yourself as someone who MUST accomplish great things for His glory.

GOD'S ORIGINAL PLAN

One definition of the word "wild" is "living or growing in the natural environment; not domesticated or cultivated." The definition of "expectance" is "looking forward to something, especially with eagerness: anticipation, expectancy, expectation." *Wild expectance* is striving to live life in the manner in which God has planned it.

At the beginning of Creation, man lived in the natural environment of Eden with God. In that setting, nothing held back man's expectations of God; everything and anything was possible. *Wild expectance* is striving to live the life God originally designed before the enemy polluted humanity's environment with sin. Daily, we must strive to return to strengthen our relationship with God—that means living every day with an expectation that God is going to do big things through you and for you. The God of miracles wants to actively do miracles in your life, use you to be a blessing, and elevate your influence to impact the world for the Gospel. The belief that God has a *Jeremiah 29:11* life for you filled with adventure and excitement is real and obtainable: "For I know the plans I have for you, declares the Lord, plans for welfare and not for evil, to give you a future and a hope."

In his book, *Making Jesus Lord*, Loren Cunningham, founder of Youth With A Mission (YWAM), shares about a time he prayed with *wild expectance* over his life: "In 1975, I was praying and thinking about how we could turn the world around for Jesus. A list came to my mind: seven areas. We were to focus on these categories to turn around nations to God. I wrote them down and stuck the paper in my pocket:

WILD EXPECTANCE IS STRIVING TO LIVE THE LIFE GOD ORIGINALLY DESIGNED BEFORE THE ENEMY POLLUTED HUMANITY'S ENVIRONMENT WITH SIN. DAILY, WE MUST STRIVE TO RETURN TO STRENGTHEN OUR RELATIONSHIP WITH GOD— THAT MEANS LIVING EVERY DAY WITH AN EXPECTATION THAT GOD IS GOING TO DO BIG THINGS THROUGH YOU AND FOR YOU.

1. Home
2. Church
3. Schools
4. Government and politics
5. Media
6. Arts, entertainment, and sports
7. Commerce, science, and technology

The next day, I met with a dear brother, the leader of Campus Crusade For Christ, Dr. Bill Bright. He shared with me something God had given him—several areas to concentrate on to turn the nations back to God. They were the same areas, with different wording here and there that were written on the page in my pocket. I took it out and showed Bill. Amazing coincidences like this happens all the time when Christians listen to the still, small voice of the Holy Spirit" (Kindle Location 1658 – 1669 of 1976).

This list has gone on to become known as the Seven Mountains of Influence: family, economy, government, religion, education, media, and entertainment. Living a life of *wild expectance* means expecting God to use you—YES, YOU—in these spheres to shift cities, states, and even nations, all while having balanced time for family and fun. It's not a promise of a storm-free life but that He will be with you in the storm and get you through it safely. Whether we live in a rural village in Haiti or on the streets of Vietnam, we can shift our environment towards the Gospel. Whether we're in Beverly Hills or Capitol Hill, we should live with the expectation that God wants to use us to impact those around us for the Gospel. I hope the many stories of *wild expectance* from my life will help challenge and encourage you to believe that anyone can think bigger and do more in their life.

My obedience to God and my willingness to have a *wild expectance* has led to exciting stories I hope will inspire you throughout this book.

THIS IS YOUR TIME

My life has had its fair share of ups and downs. There were times when I had extreme needs, while at other times, I have been able to meet the extreme needs of others. I think it's great to experience both sides of the coin. Do you agree?

It is my prayer that the adventures shared in this book will help inspire you to live the life to which you're called. As you continue reading, I'm excited to dive deeper into what God has taught me through these wild experiences and how you can apply them to your life too.

Rest assured that on this journey, you will experience numerous tests, temptations, and battles. When you're in those moments, always remember this: great tests produce great testimonies. Continually pass your tests so that you can keep graduating to greater levels of success. Remember, as God leads us, we don't have to settle in the middle of the storm. He's a good God, and He wants us to live a balanced life full of blessings for ourselves and those around us. God doesn't change. Therefore, let us be reminded of what James 1:17 says, "Every good gift and every perfect gift is from above, coming down from the Father of lights, with whom there is no variation or shadow due to change."

I'm excited that you've already started your journey of *wild expectance*. It's evident by your decision to read this book. However, as you continue to walk out this wild journey with God, things won't be perfect, but if you persevere, it will be worth the endurance.

CHAPTER 04

GOD-INSPIRED GENEROSITY

W OW, *how can they afford to give everything away for free?* I thought to myself. I was attending Keith Moore's church in Branson, Missouri, with my friend's parents for a conference. Usually, churches make you pay for physical copies of sermons, music, and DVD series; but at this church, visitors did not have to pay for anything in their store because the Lord had told the pastor to give it all away. Any family could get up to three items each time they came to church, and a single item might be a 20-set DVD series. What made the church's free store even more incredible was that they mailed copies of any of their products to anyone, anywhere in the world, AND they covered the shipping costs.

Keith Moore was a very gifted teacher. He used to teach at a Bible school and had amassed countless topics such as healing, faith, hearing the voice of God, thanksgiving, the list goes on. If there was a theme in the Bible, he probably had a series on it (if you're interested in getting access to any of these resources, just visit his ministry website at MooreLife.org. Everything is available online to download).

I vividly remember sitting there in service, minding my own business, and reflecting on how it was possible for this church to sustain giving everything away. At that moment, the Lord spoke to me very clearly and said, "Give Me *that* check. That's how."

To clarify, I had just graduated from Missouri State University and was preparing to do the most daring thing in my life: move to Los Angeles and work for free. I didn't have any money. I was broke. I was less than broke because I had my student loans along with having no money and no prospect for financial support. I was excited that my uncle had just given me a check for $500 as a graduation gift, and now God was telling me to give it away! I was especially concerned about giving up my check because my father's side is Jewish, and this uncle wanted nothing to do with Christianity.

"I can't give that away. That's my baby!" I pleaded with God. "That's all I got!" In the voice of a famous evangelist I often listened to, I heard God's response: "That's *all* I want."

Sometimes God can speak to us through situations that are familiar to us. Have you ever been in a situation when God told you to do something crazy, irresponsible (in the world's eyes), or incomprehensible? Did you doubt that God was speaking to you at that moment?

All the negative attacks from the enemy immediately bombarded my thoughts:

"You're not hearing from God."

"You can't give that! Your uncle is going to find out and never give you money ever again."

"How are you going to survive out in Los Angeles without any money?"

"Your uncle is going to see that the check was cashed by a church!"

I got up and went to the bathroom and began splashing water on my face, trying to figure out what I was going to do. *Why, oh why, didn't I just cash this check when I had the chance!* I thought to myself. When I returned to my seat, I saw the ushers passing the offering bucket to my friends. I looked to see if God had spoken to them too, but they just passed the bucket to me.

This was the moment. I knew God was convicting me to give away the check. My ministry was over—bankrupt before it even started! But nonetheless, I had to do this. I had to be obedient to God. Remembering from my business law class that I could just sign over the rights to a check, I pulled out my wallet and looked at the check one last time. I then signed it and placed it into the basket.

Perhaps you can relate to my story. Have you ever had an experience in your life when God told you to give money away to a ministry or individual? I'm not talking about giving under compulsion or pressure from a slick preacher who promised you the moon for a $1,000 seed; I'm not talking about the 10% tithe that you should already be giving of your income; I'm talking about giving a specific amount of money to a specific ministry or individual that God specifically directed. If God told you to do this, were you obedient, or were you too scared to do it? Did you allow greed or doubts from the enemy to stop you from doing what you knew was the right thing? Looking back, I'm so glad I was obedient to God at that moment.

THIS WAS THE MOMENT. I KNEW GOD WAS CONVICTING ME TO GIVE AWAY THE CHECK. MY MINISTRY WAS OVER—BANKRUPT BEFORE IT EVEN STARTED! BUT NONETHELESS, I HAD TO DO THIS. I HAD TO BE OBEDIENT TO GOD.

I reflect upon 2 Corinthians 9:6-8 as I write this: "...whoever sows sparingly will also reap sparingly, and whoever sows bountifully will also reap bountifully. Each one must give as he has decided in his heart, not reluctantly or under compulsion, for God loves a cheerful giver. And God is able to make all grace abound to you, so that having all sufficiency in all things at all times, you may abound in every good work." I decided in my heart that I was going to be obedient to God and sow my check. I resisted the fear coming against me and decided I was going to give cheerfully. I knew God was somehow going to intervene in my financial situation; I just didn't know how yet.

MY FIRST "EXIT"

The very next day, I received a call from someone who was interested in buying the vending business I started when I was 14. Earlier that week, I had put up an online listing to attempt to sell it. It wasn't making much money, and I was liquidating everything as I prepared for the move.

This business was important to me, and it was bittersweet to see it go. I started it my freshman year in high school. I began by buying gumball machines and placing them at local restaurants. I slowly purchased more and even had one placed in my school (the technical school next to my high school where I took marketing classes). I eventually expanded it into three-way candy machines—you know, those 25 cent machines that sell Skittles, M&Ms, Runts, and other various types of candy. When I turned 18, I officially turned that business into an LLC and continued to run it while in college. My college income primarily came from emptying my vending machines and donating plasma (giving plasma actually paid for my rent, and I still have the scar on what I called the "party arm" to prove it).

The person who called me said that he saw my ad and wanted to offer me $2,000. I thought it was possibly worth $5,000, but I recognized that half of my machines were not even placed, so his offer was probably fair. Winston advised me to take the deal because I was getting ready to move and wouldn't want to have to mess with it once I got to Los Angeles.

Ultimately, God answered my prayer of finding a buyer for my business. I was obedient in giving the $500 to the church, and the next day, I received $2,000. I was grateful for this, but the $2,000 still wasn't anywhere close to what I needed to survive in the city of broken dreams.

CHAPTER 05

THE KID IN RED

When I was 18 years old, I remember walking through the vendor tent of Crossover Music Festival in Camdenton, Missouri at the Lake of the Ozarks where I grew up. This was where I met a redheaded kid who would change my life forever.

He sat behind his booth with countless shirt displays propped up by macaroni and cheese boxes. His shirts cost $20 and were very simple. They had a single color print on them, and I knew that he couldn't have paid more than $4 per shirt. The shirts had bold statements like "Virginity Rocks," "Abortion is Mean," and "Pornography is for Posers."

I immediately looked to my left and saw another vendor in a tent directly across from the redheaded kid's booth. "How can you sell your shirts for $20 when the booth across from you is selling theirs 4 for $20?" I asked.

"Yeah, but their shirts suck!" he responded with a cocky rebuttal. To be fair, the competition was selling cheesy T-shirts consisting mostly of Christian versions of popular logos like Reese's Peanut Butter Cup. His shirts had a cause behind them, yet mine were just as cheesy as our mutual competitor's. I soon learned that I needed to build a brand to compete with this cocky 22-year-old kid. He was dominating the corner space with his countless overpriced shirts that were nearly twice the price of mine. People seemed to be wearing his bold shirts everywhere; whatever he was doing was working.

Who is this guy? I thought to myself. Not only was I selling my shirts for less, but mine had multicolored prints, which cost me more per shirt than his. I had to figure out a better business plan.

While standing at his booth, I looked down at a four-year-old newspaper clipping sitting on his table. I began to read the story of how this redheaded kid named Joe Baker combated the theory of evolution, the idea that birds and bananas were related. He battled for the removal of outdated textbooks from his high school in Pennsylvania. His story soon became one I knew well.

"You can't pass out those bookmarks anymore," 17-year-old Joe was told by the principal as he sat in his office. Joe had made countless bookmarks that said, "Top 10 things not to ask your biology teacher," and passed them out to everyone in school. His anti-evolution rhetoric had been a thorn in the flesh to the principal and some of his teachers for some time, and his latest stunt was the straw that broke the camel's back.

During his senior year, Joe was emboldening countless other students to stand up against (what Joe deemed) blatant indoctrination that was being taught in some of his classes through a textbook that taught debunked theories. The school had examples of evolution and diagrams displayed in classrooms that even evolutionary scientists did not believe in anymore, and yet the material was still being taught as fact. Joe wasn't about to be intimidated by his school.

"Everyone is passing out valentines cards this week, and you're saying that I can't pass out my bookmarks?" Joe responded to his principal.

"That's right, Joe."

"It's a violation of my constitutional rights."

"I don't care. We have been putting up with you and your mess, but this has gone too far."

"Then I will sue you for this."

"You go ahead and do that."

Following this conversation, Joe immediately left the principal's office and asked the secretary if he could use their phone. He called a lawyer he had been in touch with as heat had begun building up over the past few months.

"Do you have your principal's number?" the lawyer asked.

"No, but I can transfer you using this phone."

Leaning into the closed principal's door, Joe could hear the phone ring, and his principal answered the phone.

"If Joe has a cell phone, he will be suspended for life!" the principal exclaimed as Joe's lawyer let him know he was being sued. To provide further context to the principal's reaction, cell phones had yet to become a social norm amongst high schoolers and were banned at school. The principal was looking for an easy way to make his "Joe problem" go away.

This lawsuit made international news, and Joe was even on CNN. Joe's story launched him into international notoriety and helped Joe secure a speaking tour. He went on to sue his school for $1 and an apology. As one might expect, the state of Pennsylvania vigorously fought against Joe, but at the end of the day, Joe got his apology and his $1 check (which he never cashed). The whole process cost the state of Pennsylvania over $100,000 and created a divide between people who loved this kid's boldness and those who hated him.

If you were Joe, would you have had the audacity to be so bold? If that was your son or daughter, would you have had the strength to support them? I sometimes reflect on Joe's life and the boldness he learned from his mother. It makes me wonder, are fathers and mothers of this generation raising up families that are bold and willing to stand up for what is right even when it's hard?

Every generation needs believers who are fearlessly determined to serve Christ in their homes, schools, communities, and politics. If we avoid this responsibility in our own lives, a new generation will be raised up that neither knows the Lord nor what Jesus has done for us.

As I finished reading the newspaper clipping of Joe, I now understood why he took such a bold stance with his shirts. As we continued to talk, he learned that, unlike the other vendors, I actually lived in the area.

"Do you know any sweet jumps?" Joe asked. He was making a reference to cliff-jumping into the giant lake I grew up on.

"I know a really good rope swing I can take you to," I responded. He was immediately interested.

I invited Joe and his team (two other girls) over to my house to let them use one of my family's showers. My parents were eventually accommodating, but it took some convincing because our house was a mess, and there were some drainage problems with the main shower. My mother made Joe and his team lunch, and afterward, I took them rope swinging with my friend (a volunteer helping me who knew my brother from college). I had just met her earlier in the summer, and she had agreed to drive down two and a half hours from the St. Louis area to volunteer at my booth.

ARE FATHERS AND MOTHERS OF THIS GENERATION RAISING UP FAMILIES THAT ARE BOLD AND WILLING TO STAND UP FOR WHAT IS RIGHT EVEN WHEN IT'S HARD?

The last night to sell my shirts was a Saturday, and the festival had just finished. This was my last opportunity to make some money at the booth, and I needed all hands on deck. As I began to look around for my volunteer, I couldn't find her anywhere.

"Where is she?!" I exclaimed to myself. Just then, I saw her in the distance. She was standing outside Joe's booth holding his cardboard sign announcing their end-of-the-night promotion to all of the attendees flooding from the stage area past the vendor tents to the parking lot. "What are you doing? Get over here!" I yelled as I ran up to get her to return to my booth to do some last-minute, late-night hustling.

How could I have been so foolish? I was hanging out with my biggest competitor when the vendor area was closed, and now he had stolen my volunteer! At that moment, I never suspected Joe would eventually become one of my closest friends.

Following my freshman year in college, I decided I no longer wanted a booth at the music festival. It wasn't profitable for me from the year before, and I still had a lot of unsold shirts. Because I wasn't a vendor, I didn't have a free ticket to get into the festival, which I had the last two years. As a broke college student, I also didn't have the money to buy myself a ticket, but I believed that God would somehow provide me a ticket to go.

The summer had just started, and I received a call out of the blue. It was Joe. I hadn't spoken to him in a year (especially since he had stolen my volunteer).

"Are you going to be at Crossover?" he asked.

"I want to go, but I don't have a ticket," I responded.

"Come help me at my booth. I'm coming into town and will give you a free ticket."

The festival was just a few days away, and the Lord had just answered my prayer for a ticket! *But he's a competitor of mine. How could I do this?* I thought to myself.

"Can I sell my extra shirts and glow sticks at your booth?" I asked.

"Yes," Joe responded, "But you can only sell your shirts from my bargain bin."

The bargain bin was where he sold his discounted shirts. This played to my advantage because the shirts in the bargain bin still sold for more than what I sold my shirts for when I had my own booth. Once again, I accommodated him and his team with showers. My parents provided lunch at our house, and we tried to do adventurous stuff when the booth was closed.

After that festival, I didn't hear from Joe again until the following summer. Once again, Joe offered me a free ticket to help him with his booth.

DESTINED FOR THE ROAD

After helping Joe with his booth for two summers, he eventually convinced me to join him as he toured Christian music festivals across the nation. It was a very untraditional summer job, which I finally agreed to after continual pressure from Joe and nowhere else to go. It wasn't my first choice; it wasn't my second choice; it wasn't even my third choice. I tried to get a traditional summer job in finance like my cousin, who went to an Ivy League school but was instead met with closed door after closed door. Eventually, I came to the conclusion that because I couldn't land any other job, God might want me to tour Christian rock festivals.

Joe said that he would cover all the lodging, travel, and festival costs associated with touring and that we would be doing exciting things like rock climbing between events. I had a competing business, and assisting him on tour was not a paid position. Being an entrepreneur, I finally agreed to work with him only if he continued to let me sell my existing inventory in his "bargain bin" and released me to sell glow bracelets at night.

Little did I know, saying "Yes" to his offer also meant sleeping in the dirt, cooking soup on halogen lamps, and being harassed by other vendors. Joe's unorthodox marketing methods, mixed with the edginess of his shirts, were a recipe for disaster; this made us an easy target from other vendors who were either jealous of our success or offended by our shirts and aggressive sales strategies.

In hindsight, I would never have done many of those marketing ploys today. We were young, immature, at the top of the sales food chain, and we were having the time of our lives. I can understand why some of the other vendors were mad at us for using megaphones at our booths and for giving out "shirt samples."

We would cut up shirts into little strips and place them in sample cups along with a safety pin so attendees could pin a sample to their shirt to "try it out" before they purchased. It was brilliant marketing, but our competitors didn't like this, especially because we sometimes gave samples out in the walkway in front of our booth, which helped divert people over to our table and away from other vendors.

> **LITTLE DID I KNOW, SAYING "YES" TO HIS OFFER ALSO MEANT SLEEPING IN THE DIRT, COOKING SOUP ON HALOGEN LAMPS, AND BEING HARASSED BY OTHER VENDORS.**

As difficult as it was at times, touring Christian music festivals was an amazing season the Lord directed me into. Sometimes when God directs us, it doesn't make sense until years later. God clearly directed me to take this crazy summer job, knowing that it would lay a critical foundation for future opportunities to come.

Don't compare yourself to others when it comes to choosing a job or career path. God will direct you into the right path even if it's unconventional and completely different from societal norms. Don't be afraid to be different. No one will change the world by being just like everyone else.

CHAPTER 06

ROCK FESTIVAL HUSTLE

Joe said he laughed in my mother's face as she dropped off thousands of glow bracelets at his booth at Crossover Music Festival. This was now my second summer touring Christian rock festivals with Joe. I was in Kentucky at the time, working at a different festival.

"I'm trusting God that Bryan is going to be able to sell glow bracelets at Creation Music Festival," she said confidently.

"*No one* sells glow bracelets at Creation," Joe retorted and laughed.

Creation Music Festival took place in Pennsylvania and was known by many as the largest Christian music festival in the world at that time. You had to have approval for all your products six months or more in advance. My mother had no clue that on the front page of the vendor packet, it said Creation held the exclusive rights to sell glow bracelets and light products. Any vendors caught selling products similar in nature would be kicked out of the festival. Joe knew this rule well, and he wasn't trying to be disrespectful to my mom. He just knew that what we were believing God for was essentially impossible. Any of the countless vendors would have loved to sell glow products at Creation, but that wasn't going to happen.

It wasn't that Creation was malicious in making this rule; they had made thousands of dollars in the past selling glow products and used these sales as a way to offset other festival expenses. This rule (and others) were established to protect the festival, especially when dealing with 50,000+ attendees and countless vendors competing to sell their products.

Normally, my mother would have just given me the bracelets, but I wasn't even at my hometown music festival. There were two festivals taking place over the same weekend, so we had to divide our team. You might ask, "why didn't you just work at your local festival?" I don't want to talk about it, but let's just say I wasn't happy.

To compound my frustration, I learned that the bus that was going to take me from Missouri to Kentucky sold more seats than available, so when I arrived with my paid bus ticket, there weren't any seats left. Thankfully, my friends graciously drove me over 8 hours to Ichthus Music Festival from Springfield, Missouri.

I had just finished donating my $500 graduation check to the church, and though my business had sold for $2,000, I still had to figure out how I was going to survive in Los Angeles. My rent and utilities alone were going to be nearly $1,000 per month for a single room in a three-bedroom, one-bath house (this was a good deal). To provide context, I was paying just $200 plus utilities for the master bedroom and my own bathroom during my senior year in college. Compared to that, the LA housing prices were astronomical.

Despite my circumstances, I had to figure out how to convince all eight music festivals we were about to tour to let me sell glow sticks at their events. Typically, this approval process is done ahead of time, and if someone else already had the rights at the smaller festivals, that would put a wrench in my fundraising plan. I could probably make a few hundred dollars at the smaller festivals, but to be truly successful, I had to get Creation to approve my selling rights.

The summer prior, I had impressed Bubba, another vendor who was absolutely amazed as I hired kids who would sell glow bracelets on my behalf. He watched in amazement, festival after festival, as these kids brought me wads of cash while I worked behind the booth selling shirts for Joe.

If a kid couldn't afford one of our shirts, I would tell them that they could sell glow bracelets for me and that after each five they sold, they could get one free, sell it, and keep the money. The deal meant if they sold $100 worth of glow bracelets, they would be given $20 worth of additional glow bracelets which they could sell and then give back to us for a shirt.

I would train teams of kids to go into the crowd and sell these with varying levels of success. The kids had a great time and were given an opportunity to make money. I was not worried if they would steal from me because the bracelets only cost 4 cents. If they brought back just one sale, it would cover the cost of any stolen bracelets. The process was simple: I would give the kids three bracelets each to sell. If they brought me back $3, I would give them another two to sell. In exchange for their second batch of sales, I would then give them batches of five to sell, plus a free one.

Bubba understood that I had a unique gift that was repeatable at events across the country. Fast forward a few years, and I now needed to get the approval to sell these bracelets at Creation. Bubba conveniently worked at Creation along with running his own booth. He knew the organizers, one of the reasons being that he ran Uprise, another Christian Music Festival that took place in the same state. I asked Joe and Bubba to advocate for a meeting with whoever was in charge of the vendors on my behalf. As impossible as it may have seemed, I was desperate and needed Creation to say yes to my unlikely plea. Finally, I somehow got the green light that one of the heads of the festival was willing to meet with me. Joe was surprised and said this was like getting a private meeting with the mayor on Election Day.

Within the hour, one of the heads of the festival walked through the vendor tent to speak with me:

"I want to talk about selling glow bracelets at the music festival," I inquired.

"Where are they at?"

"In our van."

"And they better stay there, you understand? You will be kicked out otherwise," he aggressively said before promptly walking away.

My dream of selling glow bracelets was utterly crushed. But God can do the impossible even when the door is closed, and it seems as though all hope is lost.

Have you ever wanted something so badly, something that you thought God was calling you to, only to be met with great disappointment? Did you give up? Did you get angry with God? Or did you keep fighting and standing in faith, knowing that this closed-door would eventually lead to an opening?

I later learned that the man I had spoken with was not the head of the festival after all. Instead, he was in charge of the vendor area. He had been trained on Creation's strict policy regarding the sale of glow products and had responded accordingly. News that I had spoken with the wrong person meant there was still a glimmer of hope left. A representative of the festival later apologized for that unfortunate interaction.

I learned that the person I was supposed to meet with was in a private trailer down the hill next to the main stage. He had layers of security around the trailer, as well as a fence. I was able to make it through the first layer of security, but as I approached his trailer, his representatives told me that he wasn't interested and reaffirmed what the person earlier had said about my inability to sell glow sticks at the festival.

"He wants to meet with me," I said.

"No, he doesn't. He is busy," the representative retorted.

I was not going to take no for an answer. I didn't care what this volunteer security person said. *I was going to meet with this guy.* After all, the volunteers who were running the booths were not doing their job selling the bracelets; they were just sitting at the tables and were not engaging the attendees.

"Just go back and ask him," I pressed on.

Finally, the volunteer left for a moment before returning with a surprise on her face.

"You're right. He wants to see you."

As I entered the private trailer, I began to plead my case.

"I'm raising money for missions to move out to Los Angeles and do campus ministry at UCLA," I explained. "May I sell glow bracelets here? I will give you 50% of everything I sell."

"Okay," he responded. "But you don't have to give me 50%; I only want 25%. Additionally, I will sell you all our existing inventory at cost. You can also sell them in the crowd, and if anyone else tries to sell them, we will kick them out."

I knew I couldn't squander this opportunity. This deal was a miracle, and Joe couldn't recall a time when Creation had ever given this opportunity to a competitor. I proceeded to recruit a sales team to help me go through the crowd and sell. Each team had a vendor pass from our company so they wouldn't get kicked out. On the last night of the festival, I returned to the trailer by the main stage to settle what I owed. He was shocked at my success. He recouped his inventory costs and made a lot more for the festival than if he had stuck to their strict glow stick policy.

"Can I sell these next month at Creation Northwest?" I asked.

"Sure, we will give you the same deal there."

Creation had a smaller festival on the West Coast in Washington taking place a month later, and he agreed to give me the exclusive rights to sell there as well.

Ultimately, all the existing vendors had to give Creation 30% of everything they sold, while my business received a 5% discount, and my team was allowed to sell stuff in the crowd (something no one else was allowed to do)! Perplexed, other vendors who knew me began to ask me how I got the rights to do that. After all, I likely profited more than many of the other booths.

MY DREAM OF SELLING GLOW BRACELETS WAS UTTERLY CRUSHED. BUT GOD CAN DO THE IMPOSSIBLE EVEN WHEN THE DOOR IS CLOSED, AND IT SEEMS AS THOUGH ALL HOPE IS LOST.

What the other vendors didn't understand was that this supernatural favor was due to my obedience in generosity a month earlier. I am firmly convinced that if I had not been obedient to God and sown my $500, I would not have had this opportunity. At that moment, $500 was like the widow sowing her last mite. I am grateful that my mother was a generous woman and that she taught me how to give cheerfully to others. She sowed into many ministries, and it was through her actions that my brother and I learned to give to the Gospel.

PRACTICAL GENEROSITY

We, as Christians, are called to be generous yet balanced with our giving. Although sowing and reaping is an important topic, many times, this is focused exclusively on how we should sow our finances into the Kingdom of God. While this is a foundational discipline, sometimes, there is a lack of practical application for the other half of the equation. Some Christians are not taught the practicalities of reaping.

I believe God will bless our generosity in both this world and the next. However, there is usually an action we have to take to reap the benefits of our generosity here on Earth. That action may be tied to God's leading, so it's crucial that we learn to hear His voice.

> AS YOU EMBARK ON YOUR OWN EXCITING JOURNEY OF GENEROSITY, REST ASSURED THAT GOD'S BLESSINGS ARE NOT ONLY MONETARY. WE'RE BLESSED IN OUR RELATIONSHIPS, EXPERIENCES, HEALTH, AND EVEN IN THE JOY OF GENEROSITY ITSELF.

As you embark on your own exciting journey of generosity, rest assured that God's blessings are not only monetary. We're blessed in our relationships, experiences, health, and even in the joy of generosity itself. Regardless of who we are, generosity is non-negotiable to a faithful follower of Christ.

I'm reminded of what Dr. Siddiki once told me regarding this topic. In prayer, God once told him, "The people's giving will never meet your needs. Your giving will meet your needs." If you have a drastic need, consider going out of your way to meet the drastic need of someone else.

Regarding the practicality of reaping, if a farmer never went out and reaped his field, whatever he sowed would not matter; he would not receive a harvest because he only did half of his responsibility. We're responsible for both sowing and reaping, which are two different actions. For example, what if I was obedient to God in giving my $500 check, but I hadn't positioned myself to reap an increase? It is possible that I could have missed out on my harvest. Thankfully, we serve a good God that can always reroute our harvest when we make mistakes, but when we step out of alignment, it can cause unnecessary delays.

Therefore, we must go out, plow our fields, and when it's springtime, we must be ready to reap our harvest. Reaping is work; while each person's field may look different, we all have fields in our lives to tend to. Maybe your plowing means reading books about business; maybe it means getting a college degree; it could also mean finding a mentor who is successful in your dream field; it might even mean going above and beyond at your current job.

Whatever your plow looks like, after you sow, you have to take action when it's harvest season and apply what you have learned. For me, taking action meant buying thousands of glow bracelets, having the faith and boldness to get the rights to sell them, and then actually making the sales. I wouldn't have been successful if I skipped one of these steps:

1. I had to be sensitive enough to God to recognize that *He* asked me to give away my check.
2. I had to be obedient and actually give up the check.
3. I had to have faith that I was going to be allowed to sell glow bracelets at Creation.
4. I had to match that faith with action by purchasing enough inventory to sell.
5. I had to have the boldness to pursue this opportunity even when the door looked closed.
6. I still had to do the work of selling in the crowd after long days of working at Joe's booth.
7. I had to have the confidence to ask for the opportunity to sell at the other festivals.

Regardless of your circumstances, God is excited for you to experience the joys of generosity. Whether you're a missionary living by faith or running a multimillion-dollar business, God desires that you embrace a lifestyle of generosity and continually put Him first with your finances.

CHAPTER 07

SUMMER STORMS

As Joe and I toured Christian rock festivals together, we spent our down-time rock climbing outdoors across the United States. Since our tour was coast to coast, we were able to find a way to climb at many of the top climbing destinations across America. Because of this, I can open any climbing magazine and likely see an area I've climbed at. It was exciting to be able to climb at iconic places such as Yosemite in California, Devil's Tower in Wyoming, Mount Moran in the Grand Tetons, and the Needle's Eye near Mount Rushmore (which I fell 30 feet upside down on before my rope caught me).

Our summer tours and climbing adventures would culminate into a 1-2 week epic climbing trip at the end of each summer. This particular summer, the one right before I moved to Los Angeles, was a two-week trip into the Wind River Range in the backcountry of Wyoming. We were climbing in a beautiful area called the Cirque of the Towers and around Deep Lake. Getting there required a grueling 8 ½ mile hike, half of which was uphill. Joe, myself, and others from the tour carried in two weeks' worth of food and what felt like enough equipment to summit Everest. Before we could begin the hike, we had a two-hour drive down a gravel road starting from a town in the middle of nowhere.

"We're the only county in America that doesn't have a stoplight," one of the locals boasted as we prepared to go in. He complained the next year when the town finally installed one.

Not too long after we arrived at basecamp, it looked like our entire trip was in jeopardy. Though it was the middle of August, it began to snow. The elevation was so high here that snow could be found on some of these mountains year-round.

"This storm could last for days. There's no way we can climb tomorrow," Joe said.

"Let's just pray against this weather," I suggested.

"I remember when a storm like this came in when I climbed here with my brother. We were stuck in our tent for a week. There is no way this will clear up," Joe responded, discouraged.

A SIMPLE FORMULA

My confidence in praying against the weather came straight out of the Bible. In Mark 4:35-40, the disciples were dealing with their own storm while Jesus was asleep at the bottom of the boat. When Jesus awoke, he rebuked the storm, and it ceased. "Why are you so afraid? Have you still no faith?" Jesus reprimanded his disciples. His followers should have known better. They had walked and talked with Jesus and had already seen His miracles. Regarding praying against weather, you might be thinking to yourself, "but I'm not Jesus." Jesus graciously shares the same kind of authority He operated in while walking the Earth with us as believers. Jesus actually expects us to do greater things than He did. Jesus said this in John 14:12: "Truly, truly, I say to you, whoever believes in Me will also do the works that I do, and greater works than these will he do because I am going to the Father."

My faith gave me the audacity to believe the words of Jesus. I reasoned that if Jesus was able to pray against the storm and cause it to cease, then it was within all plausibility for us to pray and believe.

The concept was math—plain and simple. I understood this, even though I was never really good at math. I took college algebra in high school not because I was an overachiever but because I was too scared to take it in college. On my first day of business statistics class during my sophomore year in college, the teacher referenced a symbol I had never seen before (it was a sigma). I never got a Master of Business Administration (MBA), partly because I was terrified of the Graduate Management Admission Test (GMAT). Hopefully, one day, I'll get an honorary MBA from a college dean who reads this book—preferably from a prestigious east coast school (but seriously, if you're a dean, let's talk). In my experience, it was easier to make a million dollars than to pass that forsaken GMAT.

In high school, I decided that I was going to take math on my own terms with my own teachers. I heard it was easier to take college algebra in high school and then transfer the credit to my university. Then, leading into my senior year, the college algebra teacher died the week before classes started. It was a very tragic and unexpected loss to our community.

The temporary replacement was the same teacher I had for Algebra I and Algebra II. This meant I had the same teacher three years in a row for math class! When the time came for me to take my college algebra final, I received an "F." Although the final was worth at least 20% of my grade, my teacher graciously gave me a "B" in the class.

> **MY FAITH GAVE ME THE AUDACITY TO BELIEVE THE WORDS OF JESUS. I REASONED THAT IF JESUS WAS ABLE TO PRAY AGAINST THE STORM AND CAUSE IT TO CEASE, THEN IT WAS WITHIN ALL PLAUSIBILITY FOR US TO PRAY AND BELIEVE.**

Clearly, I had not earned a "B." When I asked her why she did that, she responded that she had the flexibility to make the final worth less on a case-by-case basis. *See,* math teachers, on *my* terms! Thanks, Mrs. Rowe! I worked hard and actually tried to learn the material, but it just wasn't working out. It's not *you,* math; it's me.

One formula I recall from algebra was if A was bigger than B, and B was bigger than C, then surely A was bigger than C. Call me crazy, but if our prayers were an equation, they might look something like:

Jesus's Prayers > Storm (Matthew 8:26)

Our Works > Jesus Works (John 14:12)

Our Prayers > Storm (Mark 11:23-24)

"You can't do that!" a team member complained.

"Yes, I can. It's math!"

"What about the farmers? You can't just pray against this weather; it will harm them!"

I reflected on his argument. God was unable to cause this storm to relent because farmers needed the rain. This sounded like a cop-out answer to justify his lack of faith and experience. I responded, "I believe that God has the ability to provide rain for the farmers while at the same time giving us good weather so that we can climb."

Some of the team members, along with Joe, were in disbelief and began making fun of me. I strongly sensed that the Lord was speaking to me at that moment. I felt that I had to get our team together and pray against this storm so that we could climb the next day. I believe God doesn't just want to help us in the serious moments of life, but even in the practicalities of everyday living. We wanted to go rock climbing and didn't want our trip ruined by bad weather. As the weather continued to worsen, it looked like prayer was the only solution.

I was so mad at my friends for mocking me and their lack of faith that I thought about walking down the hill and praying for a blizzard. Then, we wouldn't be able to climb tomorrow or ever! Our entire trip would consist of snow days where we slept in, made snowmen, and huddled around the fire freezing. I wanted to pray in the snow so badly, but I decided to resist.

"I think we're supposed to pray together against this storm," I insisted.

Finally, I was able to convince two others from our group to relent and pray with me. These two friends agreed because they were willing to believe my crazy idea that prayers could actually change situations (including the weather). It wasn't the others' fault that they thought I was nuts; no one had ever told them this was possible.

When pastors, teachers, and evangelists stop preaching about the power of prayer, our spiritual authority on the Earth, and the necessity of faith, a generation will rise up who won't believe. I believe this because I've witnessed faithlessness firsthand from my friends who weren't taught the authority we have as believers in Christ when we pray.

EMBRACING CHILDLIKE FAITH

I've seen ministers try to pour water on people's childlike faith. Maybe these pastors had a bad experience, or God didn't answer a big prayer. Perhaps these challenges led them to have hardened or broken hearts so badly that they decided to project their pain onto other people's faith under the guise of "balance." Or, maybe they were afraid of their reputation and being connected to someone who had faith that was bolder than theirs. They may have thought, *What if they are wrong? How will that reflect on me as their pastor or friend?*

To that type of pastor, I would retort, "Just because God didn't speak to you, that doesn't mean that He didn't speak to them." Are you someone who has the faith to believe in the middle of the storm? Or are you guilty of tearing down someone else's faith to justify your lack thereof:

"You can't believe God for that."

"That's dangerous having hope for that; you're setting yourself up for disappointment."

"You are living in a pipedream."

You shouldn't share every dream God gives you with others. Look at what happened to Joseph in Genesis 37. God had given Joseph two dreams, and when he shared these with his family, it resulted in his brothers selling him into slavery out of jealousy. I'm not saying that you shouldn't share your dreams with your family because you probably should. However, some people will always try to find a way to spin things negatively. Many times, I don't tell those people what God is doing in my life because

> **I BELIEVE GOD DOESN'T JUST WANT TO HELP US IN THE SERIOUS MOMENTS OF LIFE, BUT EVEN IN THE PRACTICALITIES OF EVERYDAY LIVING.**

they will try to thwart it with their negative words and emotions. Don't cast your pearls before swine (Matthew 7:6), even if that person is a Christian.

Are you guilty of justifying your lack of faith? Have you been the person who has torn down someone else's faith? If so, take this moment to repent and message an apology to the person you may have hurt. Take a break and do this now. The rest of this chapter can wait. If you don't have anyone to apologize to, take a moment to instead send a random message of encouragement to someone.

— Take A Moment To Message Someone Now —

Our decisions, whether good or bad, affect other people. James 3:1 teaches us how teachers will be treated harsher at the judgment when we stand before God to give an account of our life. I take this Scripture very seriously, as I don't want to be the person who causes someone else to stumble.

PRAYER ACTUALLY WORKS

I gathered with the two team members outside our camp and led a simple yet powerful prayer against the weather. It went something like this:

> *"Father God, we come together in agreement to pray against this storm that is preventing us from climbing tomorrow. In the name of Jesus, we command this storm to cease, for the weather to clear up, and for us to be able to climb with no problems. Thank you, God, for these things in the name of Jesus, amen."*

Matthew 18:19 teaches if two of us agree, it will be done. We were in agreement and prayed with faith that our prayers would change the environment. It wasn't instant, but within an hour, we noticed a legitimate, positive change in the weather. The next day, the weather had cleared up well enough that we no longer had to hide in our tents.

Joe was caught on video making this statement right before we roped in: "I appreciate Bryan Citrin's theology, his prayer life, and his ability to rebuke the storm, because yesterday this did not look possible."

Although not all of my prayers have come to pass, I have never ceased praying. Regarding the area of prayer, I once heard it put this way: not everyone got saved at Billy Graham's meetings, but did that mean he should have stopped preaching about salvation?

You might be thinking to yourself, "I've prayed for certain answers before, and nothing happened." I can relate, but I also believe that if you don't pray at all, then you are guaranteed to miss all of the answers to your prayers. I would rather pray 50 wild prayers and get ten of them answered than pray ten and only have two answered. Clearly, there has to be more to Matthew 18:19 because I don't know anyone who has ever batted 100% in their prayer life except Jesus.

Scripture tells us in James 4:2-3, "...You do not have, because you do not ask. You ask and do not receive, because you ask wrongly, to spend it on your passions." In other words, if your motive is wrong in your prayer, then you likely will not receive the answer you desire. When praying, you must first seek the Kingdom of God and develop the mindset that Jesus asks of us in Matthew 6:33.

I wholeheartedly believe God was telling me to take time out and pray about the weather. When I was obedient and prayed, God heard those prayers, and the weather cleared up.

THE WEDDING DILEMMA

Looking back, I believe that God also used that storm as a teaching moment for Joe about the power of prayer. During his outdoor wedding two years later, Joe had another opportunity to exercise his faith in the area of weather. This time his reaction was the exact opposite of how he responded in the backcountry of Wyoming. On the morning of his marriage ceremony, the weather did not look promising. For months, Joe and his soon-to-be-wife, Ann, had been planning this gorgeous wedding right in front of Sylvan Lake at Custer State Park in South Dakota; now, everything they had planned and dreamt for was at risk.

When Joe noticed that there was a storm coming in, I was the first person he came to for help. Instead of me suggesting that we pray, it was his suggestion. It was actually a desperate plea that I would pray the storm away! I told him that we both had the authority in Christ to pray. We then prayed together in agreement against the bad weather and thanked God in advance. God answered our prayers yet again, and Joe and Ann were able to fully experience the wedding of their dreams.

Later that evening, the wedding DJ turned on intense music as I quickly emerged from the woods in a gorilla suit. I ran along the side of the building, banging on the windows before jumping through an open window and running on all fours straight to the dance floor. Once there, I had a dance-off with one of the groomsmen and proceeded to breakdance before eventually being shooed away back into the woods. At that moment, I had fulfilled both Joe and Ann's desire for me to breakdance in a gorilla suit at their wedding—that was my wedding gift to them, and they loved every minute of it.

"Do monkeys bite?" Joe's niece innocently asked her mother as she watched in amazement.

You may be wondering, why did I own a gorilla suit? While touring rock festivals in a van one day, Joe and I thought it would be funny to purchase one. We were always looking for creative ways to get attention at our booths. Through this, we learned that gorillas are great fundraisers (especially when raising money to get our first mobile sonogram unit for what would eventually become Save the Storks).

However, my performing as a breakdancing gorilla after the ceremony wasn't enough for Joe. Because Joe's wedding took place in front of a small lake, he wanted to have someone across the

PRAYERS IMPACT SITUATIONS EVEN IF WE DON'T SEE IMMEDIATE CHANGE.

lake dress up in the gorilla suit so that people would think they had just seen Bigfoot in the middle of the wedding ceremony. Bigfoot would then emerge later during the reception and breakdance as planned. As much as Joe wanted someone in the gorilla suit during the actual ceremony, none of his friends or family had the nerve to do that, considering how upset that would make his soon-to-be bride; but finally, a friend agreed.

"Just go in and out of the trees while we're walking down the aisle. It's far enough away that they will doubt themselves," Joe explained.

In saying this, our friend did not realize that he had seriously misunderstood Joe's request. He thought Joe was asking him to dress up and go to the bridal tent. It's a good thing another friend intervened! He took the gorilla suit, locked it in the van, and kept the key. I realized then that God hadn't just answered our prayers about the weather; He had also answered Ann's private prayers too. She didn't want any mishaps at the wedding and only wanted people to see the gorilla during the reception. Just the thought of a gorilla near the bridal tent made her so mad. To Joe's credit, he would have been mad as well had a gorilla gone anywhere near the bridal tent. Spoiling the plan actually ended up working out for everyone's benefit.

AN INVISIBLE REALITY

Prayers impact situations even if we don't see immediate change. Within Daniel 10:12-13, we are given prophetic insight into the spiritual realm in the area of prayer: "...for from the first day that you set your heart to understand and humbled yourself before your God, your words have been heard, and I have come because of your words. The prince of the kingdom of Persia withstood me twenty-one days."

There have been times when I've prayed, and nothing seemingly happened; yet, there have been other times when I've prayed and seen immediate results. Praying against the weather in the backcountry of Wyoming was one of those times I quickly saw tangible results. But sometimes, it isn't as quick, and the answer isn't what you expect. Sometimes, God answers our prayers, and sometimes we're the answers to other people's prayers. I was already aware that prayers didn't know the distance, but what I didn't expect was that over 1,000 miles away, in the middle of my climbing trip, God would begin to answer another prayer—one that would penetrate our camp.

CHAPTER 08

UNDER
THE BOULDER

We were still in the backcountry of Wyoming, and I desperately sought a Word from God. I needed some ideas on how to survive financially in Los Angeles. Sure, I had the money I made from selling my vending business and glow bracelets. God showed Himself faithful in that way, but I still needed monthly support. I knew the money I had wouldn't last. I was confident God had answers, and I just needed to learn how to hear from Him better. This desire led me to download the free teaching series 'Spirit Led Life' by Keith Moore onto my iPod to listen to it during my climbing trip. Then one evening, I sensed God wanted me to leave camp and spend the night by myself in prayer.

"That's so cool. I wish God told me to go find a cave to sleep in and pray," one of my friends told me before I left basecamp.

As I packed up my sleeping bag and prepared to find a nearby overhang to sleep under, I believed God would give me the answers I was searching for. Because that area didn't have caves, I had to settle for a broken boulder that produced an overhang instead. Once I found the right place to sleep, I set up camp and began praying. I felt like a prophet from the Old Testament and always imagined Ezekiel lying on his side under a rock overhang like mine.

"Give $3,000 to your home church back in Missouri," I softly heard in my mind.

That couldn't be God! Instead of telling me how to make money, it seemed God was telling me where to give it. I did not anticipate this response from Him. I suddenly thought of a Bible verse. I'll admit, I had to look it up because I didn't have it memorized; either it was going to be something random, or it would line up with what I thought God was asking me to do.

Has that ever happened to you? Have you ever thought God had given you a Scripture and instead learned that that was not the case? If so, hopefully, in those moments of failure, you have learned what the voice of God *does not* sound like.

While under the boulder, it was Luke 6:38 that came to mind. I immediately opened my Bible to find the verse. After reading it, I knew God was speaking to me. The verse read, "Give, and it will be given to you. Good measure pressed down, shaken together, running over, will be put into your lap. For with the measure you use, it will be measured back to you."

That next morning, I made my way back to camp and consulted with Joe on what I thought God had spoken to me. Our conversation went something like this:

"I think God wants me to give $3,000 to my church in Missouri."

"That is crazy. You can't do that. Maybe try giving $800 instead."

"I can't do that. Either I give the church $3,000 or nothing at all."

I knew that partial obedience was still disobedience. If God was telling me to give a certain amount, then I had to do it. What God told me was difficult to accept because I had just finished working hard all summer, and now God wanted me to give nearly half of my earnings away. I understood Joe's hesitancy: impulsively giving away my hard-earned money did not make sense. Looking from an outside perspective, you would think that the situation would be reversed—that God should be telling my home church to give *me* a check, not the other way around. After all, the pastor had a beautiful facility that overlooked the Lake of the Ozarks and could probably afford to bless me financially.

As much as I didn't want to give away the money, I would rather give it in obedience than withhold it and miss what God was asking of me. I desperately needed a car, and I believed that if I was obedient in giving this offering, then God would give me a car.

The thought of giving away $3,000 was really surreal to me. To think, at the beginning of the summer, all I had to my name was $500, and God had told me to give it away. Now about a month and a half later, I had around $8,000; God had provided for me in a way that was more lucrative than any Wall Street internship, and He was asking me to be generous yet again. This time, it was six times the original amount He had asked of me!

At the conclusion of that Wyoming trip, we all returned to our respective towns to carry on our "normal" lives. At that point, it seemed as if we were all living double lives. The core group who had toured together were all from different states, and none of them touched. There was a strong comradery that was built amongst us through the blood, sweat, and tears of our summer grind.

Upon my return to Missouri to make preparations for my move, I called my home church:

"I would like to schedule a meeting with the pastor."

"He's not available until next Tuesday."

"That's perfect; that's actually the exact day that I wanted to schedule the meeting."

Not only did I think God had given me a specific amount of money to give, but the specific day to do it. When Tuesday came, I drove an hour and fifteen minutes up to the Lake of the Ozark from Springfield to meet with my pastor. We updated each other on our lives, and I shared my upcoming plans to enter donor-backed full-time ministry.

My pastor had no clue about the check I had in my wallet and my intentions to donate it to the church. That meant that there was still time for me to change my mind. Maybe he would give me a check instead. Was I making the most foolish mistake of my life? Regardless of criticisms, I knew I had to submit to my convictions and give the money away.

"I think the Lord wants me to give you this," I said as I handed him the check. He stared intently at it for a moment, surprised, as he clearly was not expecting a check of this magnitude from a recent college graduate and soon-to-be missionary.

"This is the Lord," he responded. "Come back and meet with me next week, and I will tell you more."

THE WIDOW AND THE DROUGHT

Sometimes, God can provide in the most unsuspecting ways. We set ourselves up for disappointment when we box in our expectations of how God wants to bless us. Similarly, in 1 Kings 17:9, I'm sure it was awkward for Elijah to ask the widow for assistance: "Arise, go to Zarephath, which belongs to Sidon, and dwell there. Behold, I have commanded a widow there to feed you." There was a severe drought in the land at the time, and because Elijah had accurately predicted it, a lot of people had probably blamed him. There may have been countless deaths as a result of no rain. In addition to this, God had asked

WE SET OURSELVES UP FOR DISAPPOINTMENT WHEN WE BOX IN OUR EXPECTATIONS OF HOW GOD WANTS TO BLESS US.

him to go to a random widow. "She knows the drought was my fault." Elijah could have thought. "Now God wants me to steal her last bit of food before she dies?"

Surely Elijah didn't want to risk being named the "devourer of widows" that Jesus would later describe in Luke 20:47. However, God wanted Elijah to be obedient, and this was God's way of providing for both the widow and Elijah. Therefore, he had to fulfill God's command.

Following this, Scripture tells us that God commanded the widow to feed Elijah. Her obedience meant she was not surprised when Elijah showed up asking for help and that she probably had already made preparations to do so. When Elijah arrived at her home, she acknowledged her current situation and explained how she only had enough flour and oil to make one last meal for herself and her son before she died.

Despite these circumstances, she did not give in to the fear of her current situation. Though she was experiencing a real life-or-death ordeal, she remained obedient to the Lord by feeding the prophet. Because of her obedience, her jar of flour and jug of oil supernaturally lasted until the drought was over.

What do you think would have happened if she had chosen to be disobedient to God's command? Perhaps we would never know the widow's story because she would have died. From that point, what if people made up a false theology around the story and blamed God for her death? It wouldn't have been God's fault. After all, He provided her with a way of escape. Yet without proper perspective, we can sometimes blame God for things that result from our bad choices, spiritual warfare, or even random chance. Thankfully, though, the widow's story had a happy ending because of her obedience to God during a very difficult time.

THE THREE STONES

I scheduled a time to follow up with my pastor the next week. When I walked into his office again, he proceeded to tell me a profound story. My pastor said that he was trusting God for many things, which included miracles within his family and finances. There were seven things that my pastor was praying for, and God had given him direct orders so he could see them come into fruition: he was to throw seven rocks into the water, each representing one of his prayer requests. Confused, he made the decision to drive down the hill to the lake that his church overlooked. He then walked the shoreline, searching for rocks to throw.

> WITHOUT PROPER PERSPECTIVE, WE CAN SOMETIMES BLAME GOD FOR THINGS THAT RESULT FROM OUR BAD CHOICES, SPIRITUAL WARFARE, OR EVEN RANDOM CHANCE.

"No, get them from the church property," God told him.

In his obedience, my pastor made his way up the hill to find the *right* rocks. At that point, he told me how each rock he grabbed would crumble and how after searching for a bit, he was only able to find three that wouldn't fall apart. He made his way back inside and set them on his desk.

"I'm a *pastor*. Why am I gathering rocks? Am I going crazy? What am I thinking?" he asked himself, wondering if he had actually heard from God.

"Your 2 o'clock is here," his secretary told him over the phone.

"Okay, send him in."

It was me.

God had told me to give my pastor the $3,000 check two weeks earlier. At that moment in his office, the check was no longer mine. If I was disobedient, I would be stealing. In prayer, I sensed I was supposed to meet with him on that Tuesday, and I was able to walk in at his only opening. That next week, he explained to me that he had financial problems that needed to be taken care of the next day. My pastor told me how it wasn't a big deal, but if it wasn't taken care of, it would be. He needed the *exact amount* of money I had given him, and that amount had corresponded to the three stones on his desk.

God provided for my pastor, and at the same time, He provided affirmation that I truly did hear Him in that overhang near Deep Lake in Wyoming. Later on, I remember my pastor joking that he had wished he had found all seven stones before going inside.

When did God meet my pastor's needs? Was it when I finally walked into his office or when my pastor first prayed about his needs? While he was praying for his situation, over 1,000 miles away under a boulder, God was answering it through me. God had already answered my pastor's prayer request, but what if he had stopped believing? Could my pastor's lack of faith have resulted in God telling me not to show up on Tuesday? What if I had decided not to give the check? Would my decision have meant that God had forsaken him?

I believe that God will always provide for us in every situation, but sometimes, the timing of our blessing is dependent on someone else's obedience. Said another way, God provides, but He typically uses people to do so. When we disobey God's leadership, I believe there can be a delay in what God wants to do in other people's lives. Don't allow yourself to slow down someone else's blessing because of your lack of obedience. Blessings require faith on both ends: from the person who needs provision and from the person who is the answered prayer.

TWO-SIDED OBEDIENCE

I'm reminded of a story that happened a few years later when I was fundraising for one of my mission trips to Haiti. During prayer, a name came to mind of a mother who I met over the summer. I met her only once at a music festival. She prayed over me and then gave me her phone number and email so I could routinely send her ministry updates. It was nearly a year later, and I suddenly had the thought of calling her.

She answered and what she said surprised me. "God told me to give you $500 a month ago," she explained.

"I don't know God...if You want me to give him money, then he needs to call me," she bargained with God a month previously.

Because I called her, she gave me a much-needed $500 offering to use towards my Haiti trip. But what if I had chosen not to call this mother? What if I demanded, "If God wants me to go to Haiti, have her call me." I've heard of some missionaries who refuse to ask for support. They want every experience to be like the story of the three stones. Unfortunately for them, God's provision doesn't always work that way (otherwise, every missionary would be fully funded). God works hand-in-hand with both sides to answer prayers, and every situation and answered prayer is handled differently.

> **I BELIEVE THAT GOD WILL ALWAYS PROVIDE FOR US IN EVERY SITUATION, BUT SOMETIMES, THE TIMING OF OUR BLESSING IS DEPENDENT ON SOMEONE ELSE'S OBEDIENCE.**

What if I had not called this woman and instead had made an excuse disguised as faith? Remember, James 2:20 admonishes that *faith* without *works* is dead—we need both. Whether we are trusting God for a job, raise, business opportunity, or financial ministry partner, we must know that it's up to us to fulfill our part and then allow God to perform the supernatural.

GOD'S OVERWHELMING GENEROSITY

Let's return to my story of generosity towards my pastor. Not too long after my obedience in blessing my pastor, someone unexpectedly gave me $5,000. To think, within two months of my obedience in giving my $500, God continued his faithfulness by giving me a return of ten times what I had originally sowed.

I want to clarify that I'm not promising that if you give *this*, you will get *that*. I'm simply sharing my story of Spirit-led generosity and God's faithfulness to reward my obedience in this specific situation. I learned that when we generously obey the leading of the Holy Spirit, God will bless us. My obedience throughout the summer and my willingness to move to an unknown land halfway across the country increased my faith and laid a powerful foundation for exciting journeys ahead.

CHAPTER 09

A FRESH START

When I moved to Los Angeles, I was continually on the UCLA campus. I was constantly passing out invitations to our weekly services, connecting with new students, and inviting them to events. The ministry I was interning with was a well-oiled machine that was essentially running a church on campus with weekly services, prayer meetings, Bible studies, and many other activities. It was exciting to connect with some of the most brilliant students in the world. I also loved practicing English with international students every Friday afternoon and routinely meeting with professors from around the globe who had come to UCLA to do research. My involvement in the UCLA community was a full-time job and then some. The world influence this university had was astronomical.

When I made the decision to give one year of my life to missions, I had no clue I would be doing ministry in Los Angeles for nearly 12 years. I was on campus so frequently that I found it very fitting that I was unofficially featured in UCLA's 2017 World Report. I was clearly visible in my salmon-colored shorts, inviting students to our service, when UCLA published their press release titled "UCLA ranked No. 13 in the world by U.S. News and World Report" (Google search the 2017 report, and you will see me there on the left). The report evaluated 1,250 top universities across 73 countries, and UCLA was among the top 13! These were the kinds of people I had been influencing for the Gospel.

I moved to Los Angeles because I believed God had asked me to—I truly believed this. I wouldn't have given up my previous plans and desires otherwise. I read the Bible, and I believed what it said. I wanted students to have the same encounters with God that I did. I wanted them to know that Jesus died for their sins and desired to have an eternal relationship with them. I wanted them to know that they had access to physical healing, access to deliverance and access to an intimate relationship with God. But before I continue my story, I have decided to dedicate the rest of this chapter to the hope we have as followers of Jesus and what Christians actually believe. The rest of this chapter is very serious and lays a strong foundation for our faith.

HARSH REALITY CHECK

Scripture writes about the fall of Satan (also known as the Devil, the thief, the enemy, Beelzebub, and other various names) and how he deceived one-third of the angels in Heaven to rebel against God (Revelation 12:7-12 and Isaiah 14:12-15). As a result of his deception, he and his angels were cast out of Heaven to the Earth.

Jesus referenced this deceitfulness when He said that He saw Satan fall like lightning in Luke 10:18. Hell was created because of Satan's rebellion; it was not created for humans (Matthew 25:41).

In John 10:10, Jesus declares: "The thief comes only to steal and kill and destroy. I came that they may have life and have it abundantly." Similarly, in John 3:16, Jesus said, "For God so loved the world, that He gave His only Son, that whoever believes in Him should not perish but have eternal life." These Scriptures tell us that God wants us to accept Jesus' sacrifice so that we can live for eternity in peace and joy with God. The Apostle Paul reiterates the narrative that our sin separates us from God and that we deserve death, but God has granted eternal life to those who will receive it: "For the wages of sin is death, but the free gift of God is eternal life in Christ Jesus our Lord" (Romans 6:23).

Paul, through the inspiration of the Holy Spirit, writes about how we can gain access to this eternal life in Romans 10:9: "...if you confess with your mouth that Jesus is Lord and believe in your heart that God raised Him from the dead, you will be saved."

In addition to this, Paul writes in Romans 3:23 that we've all sinned and fallen short of God's standard. We can never be good enough to achieve salvation on our own accord or based on merits. Thankfully, salvation does not come from how good we are. It is through God's saving grace that we are redeemed through faith and repentance: "For by grace you have been saved through faith. And this is not your own doing; it is the gift of God, not a result of works, so that no one may boast" (Ephesians 2:8-9).

Salvation is a free gift from God that He brought to us through the life, death, and resurrection of His Son, Jesus Christ. Jesus lived the perfect life that we couldn't live. He paid the penalty of *our* sin by dying on the cross and resurrecting in three days. Through accepting Jesus as your Lord and Savior, you have eternal life.

While Jesus died so that we could experience life, demons have their own judgment coming, as exemplified in Matthew 8:29: "And behold, they cried out, 'What have you to do with us, O Son of God? Have you come here to torment us before the time?'" This Scripture confirms that demons can never be saved. Demons attack God by harming humanity. We were made in the image of God, and demons hate that. God doesn't want any human to be sent to eternal torment. Scripture tells us, "The Lord is not slow to fulfill His promise as some count slowness, but is patient toward you, not wishing that any should perish, but that all should reach repentance" (2 Peter 3:9).

> WE CAN NEVER BE GOOD ENOUGH TO ACHIEVE SALVATION ON OUR OWN ACCORD OR BASED ON MERITS. THANKFULLY, SALVATION DOES NOT COME FROM HOW GOOD WE ARE. IT IS THROUGH GOD'S SAVING GRACE THAT WE ARE REDEEMED THROUGH FAITH AND REPENTANCE

Disobedient people send themselves to eternal torment when they reject God's free gift. Jesus taught this message on many occasions. People can say this teaching is offensive, non-inclusive, mean-spirited, and bigoted. However, Jesus and those closest to Him believed this truth, and so should we. The eternal destination of our lives and everyone we care about hinges on this.

NAVIGATING AN OCEAN OF DECEPTION

The Gospel was not birthed into a man through enlightenment after deep meditation; it was not a revelation made by an angel to a select individual. There are multiple religions today as the result of "angelic visitations." The beginning of Galatians anticipates this distortion and addresses it promptly: "...but there are some who trouble you and want to distort the Gospel of Christ. But even if we or an angel from Heaven should preach to you a Gospel contrary to the one we preached to you, let him be accursed" (Galatians 1:7-8).

Religions that distort the Gospel are themselves corrupted. The deceiving angels who spread these falsehoods provide the supposedly uncorrupted truth, whether in the form of a book, tablet, or profound revelation. As a result, I believe that spiritually dry religious founders have had supernatural encounters with fallen angels and have believed their demonic lies of enlightenment. I believe the founders of prominent world religions had a void in their hearts as they searched for truth. Demonic influences moved to fill that void—a void that should only be filled by the Holy Spirit and the truth of God's love through His son Jesus's sacrifice.

However, the Bible clearly explains that demons can present themselves as angels of light in order to deceive humanity: "And no wonder, for even Satan disguises himself as an angel of light. So it is no surprise if his servants also disguise themselves as servants of righteousness. Their end will correspond to their deeds" (2 Cor 11:14-15).

One might wonder then that if we have a supernatural experience, how do we know that it was from God? 1 John 4:1-3 gives us the answer, saying, "Beloved, do not believe every spirit, but test the spirits to see whether they are from God, for many false prophets have gone out into the world. By this, you know the Spirit of God: every spirit that confesses that Jesus Christ has come in the flesh is from God, and every spirit that does not confess Jesus is not from God. This is the spirit of the antichrist, which you heard was coming and now is in the world already."

A FRESH START

Jesus' resurrection wasn't a revelation made to a select individual; instead, it was made public to over 500 people. It is a historical fact that many of the earlier believers died for their faith. The people who walked, talked, and saw the resurrected Jesus, were so convinced that He had truly been resurrected from the dead that they were willing to die for their faith—no sane person dies for a lie. Through the sovereign power of God, there have been more Bibles created than any other religious text combined. The more that the enemy and his powers of darkness try to block God's message, the more the Gospel spreads! Kings, queens, political tyrants, and countless others have tried to squash the story of Jesus over the years, but they can't because it's not just a religion—it's the truth.

Satan has worked to tempt and deceive humanity since he tempted Adam and Eve in the Garden of Eden. Despite Satan's attempts to confuse us, there are not thousands of religions with thousands of outcomes after our lives on Earth. The truth is that there is one true God, and He is the source of our salvation. God has given us free will, and if we choose not to serve God, we are instead choosing to serve one of the false religions.

HUMANITY'S SPIRITUAL HUNGER

If the Gospel Jesus preached no longer had any supernatural power, how would we combat the powers of darkness working against humanity? If Satan thought he could tempt Jesus in Matthew 4:1, in the wilderness, how much more does the enemy and his powers of darkness believe they can tempt you and me?

I believe that if the Gospel cannot quench people's hunger for the supernatural, they will look for it elsewhere. I've seen this deception occur time and time again on college campuses: students raised in religious households who were taught theories of Jesus but never learned how to develop a relationship with Him. These students were taught a cultural Christianity that was missing important components like the power of faith, speaking in tongues, and the Gifts of the Spirit, which I will write about in the next chapter. There are only two ways to tap into the supernatural: through the Holy Spirit or demonic means. Those are your only two options, and both are heavily prevalent today. Many of these spiritually deprived students leave Christianity for either agnosticism (God exists but is unknowable) or atheism (God doesn't exist at all). Others leave in search of a religious expression that both accepts and nurtures their hunger for spiritual and supernatural experiences.

I reflect on the many trips I've taken to Haiti. The people of Haiti are very spiritual, with the national religion being Voodoo. Good luck convincing a witch doctor that his or her demonic powers do not work. The locals in Haiti have seen demonic powers in action and know that there is a real power that comes from playing with darkness.

KINGS, QUEENS, POLITICAL TYRANTS, AND COUNTLESS OTHERS HAVE TRIED TO SQUASH THE STORY OF JESUS OVER THE YEARS, BUT THEY CAN'T BECAUSE IT'S NOT JUST A RELIGION—IT'S THE TRUTH.

Thankfully, Christians can use their faith to cast out darkness through the name of Jesus. This is possible through the spiritual authority Jesus allocated to his followers that is still relevant today (Matthew 10:1,8, Matthew 17:14-21, Mark 16:17, Luke 9:1).

Winston once led a witch doctor to Jesus, after which the witch doctor asked Winston to come and burn all of the Voodoo paraphernalia he had used. The former witch doctor knew that he had to break away from his old practices completely now that he had accepted Jesus into his heart.

How are we supposed to share a Gospel void of the supernatural when there are numerous other religions around the world that have unexplainable testimonies of spiritual encounters? We do so by relying on the Holy Spirit as fervently as the early church did and by sharing our faith in the empowerment of the Holy Spirit. Jesus knew the risks that we would face by sharing our faith, but He specifically told His disciples to wait in Jerusalem until they experienced the supernatural phenomenon of Acts 1:8: "But you will receive power when the Holy Spirit has come upon you, and you will be my witnesses in Jerusalem and in all Judea and Samaria, and to the end of the Earth."

However, coming from a background that teaches the full Gospel with the empowerment of the Holy Spirit does not guarantee that you will not face attacks, struggles, or eventually give in to the pull of the enemy. There are plenty of stories of people who grew up with strong Christian foundations who departed from their faith as they experienced success in business, politics, or Hollywood. The enemy plays for keeps and will do anything he can to drive a wedge between God and us, whether that be money, sex, or power.

SPIRITUAL OFFENSE AND DEFENSE

In spite of all the darkness in the world, there is hope—light casts out all darkness. The Bible is full of testimonies in which good overcomes evil. For example, Ephesians 6:16 teaches the necessity of taking up the shield of faith to protect us from the attacks of the enemy; James 4:7 teaches us to submit to God and resist the Devil, which will cause him to flee: Isaiah 54:17 confidently asserts that no weapons formed against us shall prosper.

To be clear, we as Christians are not called to take a fearful or timid stance when supporting our faith. You may think to yourself, "Maybe if I don't rock the boat, the enemy will leave me alone?" Powers of darkness have been actively working against you, your parents, your grandparents, and so forth for generations; they have been plotting against you and will continue to do so regardless of what you believe. We are reminded in Hosea 4:6 that God's people perish for lack of knowledge—but no more! You have the knowledge; now, be proactive with your time.

God needs people of this generation to rise up as dauntless prayer warriors who will influence business, the media, politics, and education for His glory. In order to rise up properly, we must not be fearful of retribution for our testimony. God will watch over us as we submit to His will.

When people think of spiritual protection, sometimes they think about Matthew 16:17-19, which affirms: "And I tell you, you are Peter, and on this rock, I will build my church, and the gates of Hell shall not prevail against it. I will give you the keys of the Kingdom of Heaven, and whatever you bind on Earth shall be bound in Heaven, and whatever you loose on Earth shall be lost in Heaven." This was the message that Jesus gave to Peter when Peter recognized that He was the Christ.

Jesus grants the body of Christ spiritual authority over the powers of darkness. Gates are defensive measures. Therefore, Matthew 16 is actually saying that the defensive measures of the power of darkness will not prevail against our attacks. When we make Jesus our Lord and Savior and make it our priority to attack the enemy, the kingdom of darkness' defenses will not last. As a result of the loss that Satan will take, politicians, business leaders, and Hollywood titans alike will have radical conversions for Jesus. Leaders from other religions will have visions of Jesus, and the truth of the Gospel message will be spread around the world.

It isn't a matter of *if* this will happen, but *when* and *how* you will participate in the mission to spread God's Word. Consider how Jesus told his disciples in Matthew 10:7-8: "And proclaim as you go, saying, 'The Kingdom of Heaven is at hand.' Heal the sick, raise the dead, cleanse lepers, cast out demons." Too many Christians are on the sidelines with an unbiblical and watered-down worldview of their responsibility; it's time to take the kingdom of darkness by the storm, and it starts by sharing your testimony with others.

A NEW BEGINNING

If you have never accepted Jesus Christ as your Lord and Savior, and want to start a relationship with Him, then today is the day for your salvation. If you are a Christian who feels distant in your faith, today is the day to rededicate your life to Christ. If either of these are true for you, please repeat this prayer aloud right now:

> *"Father God, I believe You sent Your son Jesus to live a perfect life and to die on the cross for my sins. I believe You raised Him from the dead after three days and that through faith in Jesus, I can have eternal life. I repent for any sins I've ever committed, either known or unknown.*

I forgive anyone who has ever sinned against me. I accept Your Son Jesus Christ as my Lord and Savior. I ask your Holy Spirit to come and dwell in me. Thank You for saving me. Please lead me into my God-given purpose. I pray these things in Jesus' name, amen."

It is a sad reality, but people die every day without experiencing the truth of salvation. People who choose to reject the free gift of salvation through Jesus' sacrifice default to Satan and his deceptive nature. Through the rejection of Jesus, these same people receive Satan's punishment: eternal separation from God and unending torment in the lake of fire. This outcome may sound harsh, but it is accurately supported in Scripture. God does not wish for any humans to go to Hell. This is why it is crucial that we boldly and expectantly share our testimony with others with anticipation that people will be positively transformed by the Gospel.

TOO MANY CHRISTIANS ARE ON THE SIDELINES WITH AN UNBIBLICAL AND WATERED-DOWN WORLDVIEW OF THEIR RESPONSIBILITY; IT'S TIME TO TAKE THE KINGDOM OF DARKNESS BY THE STORM, AND IT STARTS BY SHARING YOUR TESTIMONY WITH OTHERS.

We have to share our faith with others and bring them into the same relationship we have with Christ. If we do not, they will, unfortunately, be met with the fate of the fallen angels, living in eternal torment and separation from God. Here are some additional Scriptures to encourage you to prepare your testimony for others:

> "...but in your hearts honor Christ the Lord as holy, always being prepared to make a defense to anyone who asks you for a reason for the hope that is in you; yet do it with gentleness and respect" (1 Peter 3:15).

> "...preach the word; be ready in season and out of season; reprove, rebuke, and exhort, with complete patience and teaching" (2 Tim 4:2).

> "And they have conquered him by the blood of the Lamb and by the word of their testimony, for they loved not their lives even unto death" (Rev 12:11).

I'm excited that you made it this far in this book. Now that you have a strong foundation of what Scripture says about salvation, the next chapter will empower you with the Holy Spirit and teach you in-depth spiritual truths that have transformed my missionary journey. The pages to come provide an important perspective for the incredible stories that are about to unfold later in this book.

I have been blessed with the opportunity to learn from some amazing Christian leaders and am excited to share with you what they have taught me. Don't miss this next chapter. Everything I continue to share is Biblical and will equip you for more effective living. It doesn't matter what your career or faith background is. Whether you're working a corporate job, in the ministry, or a politician, whether you're a blue-collar, white-collar, stay-at-home parent, or entrepreneur, it doesn't matter. This next chapter is for you!

CHAPTER 10

UNLOCKING GOD'S POWER

"So...how did you do it?" I inquisitively asked our guest speaker Sean Smith as I drove him to the airport.

I had been a full-time missionary living in Los Angeles for a few years now, and we had just finished our weekly service at UCLA. At the end of Sean's message, he began to pray for people. However, he didn't just wrap up his sermon by inviting people to come forward for private prayer. Instead, from the front of the room, he began praying for people publicly as they sat in their seats. Instead of these people sharing their needs and asking him to come into agreement in prayer, it was as if Sean already knew some of their deepest desires or concerns. He even knew the needs of some people who would have never responded to an "altar call" if he instead invited them to come to the front of the room in response to his sermon for private prayer.

As Sean began to pray for people and prophetically speak people's prayer requests, he was even able to pinpoint certain people's specific health concerns. He would then prophetically encourage them, having knowledge about them he couldn't have known beforehand. I want to clarify that he was not publicly revealing anyone's hidden sins. Part of Sean's approach included sharing a piece of information that only God could have revealed to him to provide credibility; then, he proceeded to prophesize to them and provide encouragement about their future and God's love for them.

After he revealed a health concern of someone in the room, Sean would then have everyone near that person pray with them. Many times the person would then get healed instantly. Other times, they were healed progressively and would share their testimony with Sean at a later date. As Sean prophesied over those in the room, he actively built up many people's faith who were present. Because of this, people had faith for divine healings, which in return resulted in God healing people.

The Bible talks about the importance of faith when praying for others. At the end of Mark, Jesus taught that in His name, those who believe would lay hands on the sick, and they SHALL recover. Sean took this verse literally, as exemplified by how he ended his services.

There was no way Sean's prophecies were premeditated or an "act." I had just met one of the students he had prayed for that week, who was now experiencing his first service. I knew for a fact that Sean hadn't met with the student ahead of time because I picked Sean up from the airport, and Sean was with me the entire time. Sean's obedience to God during that service and others he did for us at UCLA resulted in students getting saved, healed, delivered, and plugged into discipleship programs in our ministry.

But how were his prophecies possible?

Sean was operating in what is referred to as the *Gifts of the Spirit*: supernatural God-given gifts that are still prevalent today and point people to Christ. Regarding this topic, you likely fall into one of three categories: either you believe these gifts still happen today (and have likely seen them in operation), you were taught that these don't happen anymore, or you have no clue what I am writing about. Please continue reading this chapter regardless of your current beliefs on this topic.

If you were taught that these gifts were not for today, I'm sorry to let you know that you have been lied to. Whoever taught you this likely did not do so out of malice but instead out of ignorance. It is probably not their fault that they mistakenly taught you a lie; they may not have known any better because someone may have lied to them too (and their teacher was also lied to and so forth).

I'm not writing this chapter to offend you. I could easily omit this entire section. To be honest, some people told me to leave this chapter out—people who believe everything I am writing about. However, I am not going to continue the lie this time by omission.

I hope you understand that I'm including this because I have a conviction that people need to know the truth regarding some important topics that are overlooked in many churches. Specifically, I'm referencing the Gifts of the Spirit and the Baptism of the Holy Spirit. You've made it nearly halfway into this book, so please hear me out. I'm not crazy. This is an important chapter that will equip you with the supernatural power of the Holy Spirit and set a valuable foundation for other wild stories to come.

I grew up under an ordained Baptist pastor who also grew up thinking the Gifts of the Spirit didn't happen today. That viewpoint changed for my pastor when he was in Baptist Bible school. One of his professors pulled him aside and prayed for him to receive the baptism of the Holy Spirit with the evidence of speaking in tongues. From that moment, my pastor was forever changed. He then would go on to pray for countless others to receive this free gift.

People are described as being baptized in the Holy Spirit when they receive their supernatural prayer language (reference Luke 3:16, Acts 1:5, Acts 1:8, and Acts 2:4). When we get saved, the Spirit comes and dwells in us, but there is a second experience, as outlined in Acts, where people receive the gift of the Holy Spirit. The early disciples were not weirded out by this experience because one of the last things Jesus told them before ascending into Heaven was that those who believed would pray in tongues: "And these signs will accompany those who believe: in My name, they will cast out demons; they will speak in new tongues" (Mark 16:17).

We should probably take seriously one of the last things Jesus said. We shouldn't ignore it or justify why this truth doesn't apply to us just because we may have a hard time understanding the context behind it.

It's important to understand that praying in tongues as a personal prayer language is different from gifts of the Holy Spirit as outlined in 1st Corinthians. The gifts in 1 Corinthians 12 manifest as the Spirit wills. It is not that some people have the gifts and others don't—it's an in-the-moment occurrence. Sean explained this as having a toolbox and the Lord providing you with different tools for different situations. But you first need to be familiar with the tools and have a desire to use them. Paul teaches us to desire these gifts in 1 Corinthians 14:1, saying, "Follow the way of love and eagerly desire gifts of the Spirit, especially prophecy."

In 1 Corinthians 12:1, Paul tells us that he doesn't want us to be uninformed about spiritual gifts. Yet that is exactly how many Christians are: they are uninformed on this topic, and they do not believe spiritual gifts exist today.

The Gifts of the Spirit are then laid out later in the chapter. Read for yourself what the Apostle Paul teaches in 1 Corinthians 12:8-10: "For to one is given through the Spirit the utterance of wisdom, and to another, the utterance of knowledge according to the same Spirit, to another faith by the same Spirit, to another, gifts of healing by the one Spirit, to another the working of miracles, to another prophecy, to another the ability to distinguish between spirits, to another, various kinds of tongues, to another the interpretation of tongues."

I'm not going to go in-depth regarding the different Gifts of the Spirit right now. There are entire books dedicated to that topic. The book *Unlocking the Mysteries of the Holy Spirit* by Dr. Larry Ollison is a great resource for further study of Spiritual Gifts.

LEARNING FROM GIANTS

Sean is a ministry giant and continually has the opportunity to learn from and minister alongside other great giants of the faith. For example, he was able to have lunch with the famous German evangelist Reinhard Bonnke, who was known as the Billy Graham of Africa. Reinhard is credited with having the largest altar call ever during one of his African crusades. I once asked Sean what were the biggest things he learned from being around these other powerful ministry leaders. I wanted to glean some of Sean's spiritual mentorship that he received from them.

In the area of revival, Reinhard told Sean that instead of believers just sitting back and waiting for a revival, it was time for believers to go take in the harvest for the Lord. Reinhard told Sean that revival was already here waiting on us, but we had to go out and preach the Gospel, win over the lost souls, and have an expectation of signs and wonders following. Reinhard clearly lived out this principle in his life. He had an estimated 79 million people come to Christ because of his ministry, and countless miracles followed his preaching during his many Gospel crusades.

In the area of the prophecy, Sean's mentor Cindy Jacobs, a prophetess to the nations, told Sean to "Prophesize into the valley in their lives. That will get their attention in the shortest time and build them up in the biggest way."

Sean knew I wanted to be used more in the prophetic and encouraged me to pray: "Lord, show me the valley in this person's life, and let me speak to it." As Sean continued to teach me about the prophetic ministry, he said, "Everyone wants to prophesize to people's mountain tops. For example, if you're good at evangelism, you can say, 'Brother, I just see the Lord is going to use you in evangelism.' That would be good, but what if someone knew the valley and the struggle and prophesied that? Wouldn't that get their attention the quickest and leave them walking away the most built up at that moment?"

HEARING FROM GOD

When we think of the voice of God, sometimes we think of an audible voice. However, when we think about it, an audible voice isn't the most efficient way to communicate. If God's Spirit is in us, wouldn't it be more efficient for God to speak to us through pictures, ideas, and thoughts in our imagination? Or even better, what about an instant knowing of something just like how Sean knew details about students in our ministry before he prayed for them? This is one of the reasons why we need to strive to keep our thoughts pure and focused on Him. Otherwise, we may overlook what God is communicating to us.

As Sean continued to share with me what he learned from ministry leaders, he suggested, "Who's to say that Jesus wasn't led by faint impressions 95% of the time?" He then said something that has stuck with me to this very day about hearing the voice of God: "The voice of God can come as a sudden awareness followed by a unique conviction," he explained. "We typically think in linear progression. If I'm preaching and then randomly thinking about some dude's spleen, maybe it's God." Sean went on to explain that God can even use our body as an instrument. If we suddenly have back pain, maybe God is pinpointing the pain of someone else in the room.

"One of the ways you unlock deeper sensitivity to this is praying in the Spirit. Whenever I'm about to minister, I pray in tongues for at least an hour in preparation. That is where I develop the intimacy and sensitivity to the Spirit of God so I can pour out what He wants to do in the service," Sean emphasized.

No minister ever told me they prayed in tongues for at least an hour before they preached, and no one else I knew operated in that kind of prophetic anointing either. Sean was clearly onto something. Most people don't draw the connection that when the Bible writes about praying in the Spirit, it's referencing praying in tongues.

"When stepping out in the prophetic, think of it as a box of tissues. When you pull out the first tissue, the second one comes out. When you pull out the second one, the third one comes out. But so many of us want to have all ten tissues metaphorically speaking before we step out," Sean continued. I thought his explanation was a good one, and it has helped me over the years as I've developed my prophetic gifting and sensitivity to the Lord. When I asked Sean what books had helped him develop in this area, he recommended the book, *Developing Your Prophetic Gifting* by Graham Cooke.

In regards to prophecy, Sean explained that one of his spiritual mentors taught him to expect to miss it at least three times while first starting. Sean continued to elaborate and said that there was no such thing as mistake-free Christianity and flowing in the Gifts. Mistakes were not optional. As you read this, let this thought be an encouragement rather than a discouragement.

Don't allow mistakes to prevent you from walking in the power God has designed to accompany your testimony. These mistakes are an opportunity to grow in your intimacy with Him. Every time you miss it, you now know what God doesn't sound like and are one step closer to accurately hearing from God. Archive each of these experiences in your memory to reflect upon later as you continue to discern the voice of God for yourself and others.

There's also no such thing as mistake-free running: first, you crawl, then you walk, then you run. What if you slapped a baby and told them never to try that again when the baby fell after trying to walk for the first time? That's what the church can do to believers who are maturing in the operation of the Gifts of the Holy Spirit. Alternatively, the church should receive grace and give grace to believers still learning to operate in these gifts.

In regards to praying for others and being used in the prophetic, we must establish boundaries to protect ourselves and others. As a general rule, do not prophesy out specific dates of when something is going to happen, do not prophesy who someone is going to marry, and do not prophesy when a couple is going to have babies. The prophetic should help affirm what God is already speaking to them. You won't always be perfect, and it's important not to set others up for extreme disappointment.

THE VOICE OF GOD CAN COME AS A SUDDEN AWARENESS FOLLOWED BY A UNIQUE CONVICTION.

For example, there are prophetic voices that have made outlandish statements in the past that have not come true, causing discouragement to those who believed the statements. Don't set yourself up for failure and avoid these types of prophecies altogether. I've heard it summed up in five simple words: avoid dates, mates, and babies.

Remember, Sean said he would always pray in tongues for at least an hour before he preached. During these times of prayer, he would develop a greater sensitivity to what God wanted to do in the service, the topics he was supposed to teach on, and at times, even be revealed things through the Holy Spirit that otherwise would have been impossible to know.

I'm reminded of what Dr. Siddiki taught me: "Praying in tongues is like laying the railroad tracks to God's perfect will for your life. There are places God wants to take you to and things He wants you to do. But you can't walk into that path until you first pray it out. There are things God wants to do in your life one year, five years, and ten years from now that have to be prayed out in the Spirit first." Dr. Siddiki compared this to the difference between weed-whacking through a thick jungle and walking on a paved path. You've already read about many wild stories in my life that came to fruition through praying in tongues, and you will continue to read about many more.

If praying in tongues is this important, then why does it seem like almost no one talks about it? Is it because it doesn't happen today? Or is it because it's so crucial as a tool for believers that the powers of darkness want to do everything they can to discredit it?

I want to clarify that praying in tongues is not a requirement for salvation but, instead, a free gift to help us along the way. Some believers alienate others by saying that praying in tongues is required for salvation. That is not true. Salvation comes through faith in Jesus Christ alone.

James 4:2 explains that *we have not* because *we ask not*, but what do we do when we don't know what to ask for? We can ask for those things by praying in tongues. The benefit of this is that you don't know what you're praying. If you did, you might not be able to have faith for it because it was such a big request, and the Bible says that when we pray, we have to pray in faith.

PRAYING IN TONGUES IS LIKE LAYING THE RAILROAD TRACKS TO GOD'S PERFECT WILL FOR YOUR LIFE. THERE ARE PLACES GOD WANTS TO TAKE YOU TO AND THINGS HE WANTS YOU TO DO. BUT YOU CAN'T WALK INTO THAT PATH UNTIL YOU FIRST PRAY IT OUT.

Additionally, the enemy doesn't know what you're praying for, so he can't stop you. You may be praying a small prayer in English, but when you pray in tongues, you are praying a bigger prayer. This unknown prayer opens the door for God to intervene powerfully in your life and the lives of others.

You may say, "Wait, I only pray big prayers in my life!" Even if you do pray big prayers by the world's standard, God's perfect will is even bigger than that! For example, in 1 Corinthians 2:9, the Scripture teaches that it has not even entered into our thoughts the good things God has prepared for us. I believe God is preparing great things for us not only in Heaven but during our time here on Earth as well. As we pray out God's will in an unknown language, at times, we are helping pray into action these amazing things for ourselves, while at other times interceding God's perfect will on behalf of others.

74

THE ENEMY'S MANIFESTO

If I was the enemy, I would do everything I could to prevent you from praying in tongues; if I was the enemy, I would send out my legion of demons to prevent people from praying in tongues before they even started. The idea of believers praying for God's perfect will without my evil army's knowledge of what they were praying for would be terrifying.

If I was the enemy, I would have to attack first. I would be afraid of a repeat of Peter's sermon in the second chapter of Acts. I would have seen the transformation in Peter's life that took place after he rejected Jesus three times, a transformation and boldness that empowered Peter to preach a powerful sermon at Pentecost, which resulted in three thousand new believers. I would have seen the boldness that took place in his life EXACTLY when he received the baptism of the Holy Spirit and began praying in tongues.

Because of these things, I would infiltrate the church with a spirit of fear. I would tell believers that they were making up sounds when in reality, they were legitimately praying in tongues. I would tell them it was gibberish and that they sounded weird. I would tell them that they were blaspheming God. I would whisper whatever lies I could to prevent them from receiving this gift. I would tempt those who received their prayer language into sin. Afterward, I would make accusations against them and justify why those who haven't yet received this don't need this tool.

I would continually whisper in your ear, "Look at those hypocrites and how they pray in tongues...why would you ever want to be like them?"

If a few people did receive their prayer language, I would flood their minds with threats and tell them they would be ostracized by their church and mission board if they were caught praying in tongues (and that is exactly what happened).

I would make it as difficult as possible to talk about praying in tongues and make it as difficult as possible for people to receive their prayer language—not because this is hard to receive, but I would play mind games with them and make them doubt everything and live in fear and anxiety. I would make the idea of praying in tongues so taboo that eventually, people would just stop talking about it. Eventually, people would begin believing this lie that praying in tongues isn't for today. They would then justify this lie by taking Scripture out of context to force Scripture to match their lack of experience.

A BOOST OF CONFIDENCE

For those who have already received this powerful gift, it is crucial that you pray in tongues every day because the enemy doesn't know what you're praying for and can't stop it. For those who haven't yet received the ability to pray in tongues, press into God more, and have a desire and *wild expectance* that you will receive this powerful gift.

I've heard the complaint that all that Pentecostals and Charismatics want to talk about is praying in tongues. What I found is that this is furthest from the truth. The sad reality is that many Charismatic believers who I've met talk about praying in tongues very little. It may have been a gift they received while they were young, but many have had very little training and education on the topic. That's how it was for me—I knew it was important, but I wasn't taught just how important it was. I remember having coffee once with someone who was about to graduate from an elite Pentecostal seminary. He had no clue just how important praying in tongues was, and he was the associate pastor of a Pentecostal church!

If you have not yet received the gift of praying in tongues, that is alright. God wants you to receive this, and I believe you will. Later in this chapter is a simple prayer for you to receive this gift. I know you will receive it because of Luke 11:13, which says, "If you then, who are evil, know how to give good gifts to your children, how much more will the Heavenly Father give the Holy Spirit to those who ask him!"

IT'S NOT BASED ON WORKS

I've seen people turned off by speaking in tongues because of people's unrighteousness. Please note that it's a free gift given to us by faith as a spiritual tool to perform a job. It's not based on how holy we are.

For example, Galatians 3:5 reads, "Does He who supplies the Spirit to you and works miracles among you do so by works of the law, or by hearing with faith."

One of the reasons a friend of mine was against speaking in tongues was because his father-in-law had received this gift but later became an abusive alcoholic. It sounds to me as if the father-in-law wasn't utilizing his prayer language but instead developed a drinking problem which resulted in him becoming a bad husband and father. That is why I believe the next chapter in 1st Corinthians talks about love. We can receive these gifts to do a job, but if we aren't following the basic tenets of Christianity (love, generosity, and obedience), it doesn't matter.

In 1 Corinthians 13:1-3, it reads, "If I speak in the tongues of men and of angels, but have no love, I am a noisy gong or a clanging cymbal. And if I have prophetic powers, and understand all mysteries and all knowledge, and if I have all faith, so as to remove mountains, but have no love, I am nothing. If I give away all I have, and if I deliver up my body to be burned but have no love, I gain nothing."

This passage of Scripture isn't discounting the value of tongues; instead, it emphasizes the importance of love. Sometimes people get offended at others' sins and end up *throwing out the baby with the bathwater*. People go on to take a later part in this chapter out of context too. I remember the first time I was challenged about this topic during my junior year in college:

"Speaking in tongues is not for today," the negative campus pastor told me.

"Had I been living a lie all these years?" I pondered.

The pastor continued to challenge what I believed. "I used to pray in tongues until someone came up to me and said I was blaspheming God in another language," this pastor continued. "Scripture says when the perfect comes, then tongues and prophecy will cease. The term *perfect* is talking about the coming of the Bible, and that's why tongues aren't for today," the pastor emphasized, trying to discourage me from practicing this gift.

He was referencing 1 Corinthians 13:8-10, which reads, "Love never ends. As for prophecies, they will pass away; as for tongues, they will cease; as for knowledge, it will pass away. For we know in part and we prophesy in part, but when the perfect comes, the partial will pass away."

I had never heard his argument before. If I was dropped on a desert island with only a Bible and no one to teach me, would I have come to this conclusion? What he said was hard to believe, especially when the next chapter, 1 Corinthians 14:39, concludes by saying, "So, my brothers, earnestly desire to prophesy, and do not forbid speaking in tongues."

Additionally, nowhere in the Bible could I find an example in which speaking in tongues was blaspheming God. In fact, some of the last words of Jesus in Mark 16:17 were: "And these signs will accompany those who believe: in My name, they will cast out demons; they will speak in new tongues."

The Bible tells us we should pray in tongues; therefore, it sounded like this pastor had a belief issue. Unfortunately, someone had lied to him and stolen his faith in this area. The enemy ran the misinformation playbook, leaving this pastor discouraged from exercising this free gift that God had for him.

The enemy ran a misinformation plan against my brother as well, resulting in him believing a lie. While in high school, someone prayed for my brother to receive the Holy Spirit, and as he began to pray in tongues alone, countless negative thoughts began to flood his mind:

"Stop doing that."

"You're just making that up."

"People are going to make fun of you."

"You're stupid."

Eventually, after a couple of weeks, he believed those lies and stopped praying in tongues or even thinking about it. He didn't think to ask others at church about the negative resistance he encountered. He instead continued to do sports, play video games, and other things high schoolers did and did not think about it again until he got involved with Chi Alpha, the campus ministry I would eventually work with.

During his senior year of college, he attended a conference with Chi Alpha. At one of the breakout sessions, the speaker talked about speaking in tongues and what my brother had experienced. The speaker then challenged everyone to do something that changed my brother's life: "Pray in tongues every day for the next 30 days, and see if it doesn't radically impact your life."

My brother took the speaker up on this challenge, and things shifted for him. I saw a very real change in my brother. Through this experience, he began to hear from God more clearly and was directed into a new career path when he wasn't originally granted a pilot slot.

Sometimes, when someone first receives the gift of praying in tongues, they are immediately discouraged by mental attacks from the enemy or those around them. This can result in their discontinuing this type of prayer. That is exactly what happened to a student in our ministry. Before he became involved in our ministry, he read a book that taught about the Holy Spirit. By himself, he prayed that he would receive his prayer language, and he did.

PRAY IN TONGUES EVERY DAY FOR THE NEXT 30 DAYS, AND SEE IF IT DOESN'T RADICALLY IMPACT YOUR LIFE.

He received this gift but didn't know anyone else who prayed in tongues. By coincidence, his girlfriend was from the same denomination as the negative campus pastor who tried to discourage me from praying in tongues. He told his girlfriend about it, who knew nothing about speaking in tongues, and she was skeptical. The student knew there was something to this because it was mentioned so much in the New Testament. However, the enemy fed into his insecurities that he was doing it wrong. Like my brother, the student battled through negative thoughts:

"I'm not getting anything out of this."

"Is it something that's important?"

"What's the point?"

"Everything is fine if I don't do this."

"Most people don't do this."

"Is this the Holy Spirit praying through me, or am I making up gibberish?"

Not too long after this experience, the thought of praying in tongues faded away, and he stopped because of his weak foundation on the subject, not realizing its purpose. Thankfully, I met him on campus later that year and was able to have an in-depth discussion with him about this topic during our fall retreat. Praying in tongues is a normal part of his life now, and he has prayed with me for other students to receive this free gift.

When I first spoke with that negative campus pastor during my junior year of college, I was naive in my Scriptural knowledge of the topic. If I had that same conversation now, I would have shown him the extensive amount of Scripture that counters his argument and backs up my experience. I would ask him if he would like to pray with me for him to reignite that gift he received so many years before.

I'm glad I had this difficult conversation with the negative campus pastor because it challenged what I believed and made me go back and really dive into Scripture. During this time, I had to decide what I believed for myself and not just what I was taught as a child.

When I experienced the baptism of the Holy Spirit with the evidence of praying in tongues during youth camp at 16, I didn't have a hard time receiving. I knew that praying in tongues was legitimate because my mother told me she prayed like this when I was around seven or eight years old. Praying in tongues was something I did throughout my whole college career, and I would especially pray like this before I prepared for the Bible study I led on campus.

Though I believed this was a crucial tool, I didn't quite comprehend the significance of my prayers until years later. I was praying in tongues at church when I believed God was telling me to move to Los Angeles. The campus pastor at UCLA was praying in tongues when I called him and said I wanted to do an internship with him.

I've noticed that those who've had the hardest time receiving their prayer language are people who have been taught against this. A friend once argued to me that any examples of speaking in tongues today were people babbling nonsense and fabricating sounds. While I'm sure there have been cases where people have made prayers up, his argument not only goes against Scripture but science.

THE SCIENCE BEHIND IT

A scientific study was done by Ivy League researcher Dr. Andrew Newberg at the University of Pennsylvania. His interest in how science and faith intersect led him to do a series of brain scans of people in prayer, meditation, rituals, and various trance states.

Although he studied multiple religions, included in his study were brain scans of Christians praying in English and then switching to praying in tongues. What he saw was so astounding that it justified a 'Nightline' episode.

The brain scan showed that the frontal lobe, the area which controlled language, lacked activity when a person was praying in tongues as compared to praying in English. When they added worship music and removed the cameras, the praying in tongues practice showed even less brain activity. If those people were just making up sounds, the results should have been more in line with one of his previous studies. His previous research showed Buddhist monks in meditation, and Franciscan nuns praying in their native language had noticeably more brain activity when compared to those speaking in tongues.

I thought this study was very interesting, and I wanted to learn more. I had the audacity to contact Dr. Newberg and interview him over Zoom firsthand about his research. He affirmed what the 'Nightline' episode had said. He brought additional clarity and said that the study was actually on monitoring the brain's activity of someone singing in tongues.

I'm not surprised with the results of his study because the inactivity from this scan matches up with what Scripture teaches in 1 Corinthians 14:14-15: "For if I pray in a tongue, my spirit prays, but my mind is unfruitful. What am I to do? I will pray with my spirit, but I will pray with my mind also; I will sing praise with my spirit, but I will sing with my mind also."

Dr. Newberg went on to explain a more unusual study he conducted. This study analyzed the frontal lobe activity of experienced mediums (psychics who claim they can talk to the dead) who said they could enter into a spiritual world and be taken over by a spirit. This study compared the brain activity of experienced mediums who wrote normally and compared it to when they entered into a trance-like state and wrote as they "supposedly" channeled deceased spirits. The results showed that the experienced mediums had a decrease in frontal lobe activity and produced more complex writings when compared to their frontal lobe activity when writing normally. From a Biblical perspective, this is the kind of result one would expect. If these mediums weren't truly becoming "possessed" as they wrote, their frontal lobe activity should have been the opposite because the complexity of what was being written required additional brain activity.

THE BRAIN SCAN SHOWED THAT THE FRONTAL LOBE, THE AREA WHICH CONTROLLED LANGUAGE, LACKED ACTIVITY WHEN A PERSON WAS PRAYING IN TONGUES AS COMPARED TO PRAYING IN ENGLISH.

I want to clarify that when mediums practice activities like this, they are not actually communicating with our deceased loved ones but are instead communicating with demonic spirits who desire to lie, deceive, and manipulate us. The results of this study reaffirm what I wrote about in the previous chapter regarding the very real spiritual battles we are all facing. Remember, you can get access to the spiritual realm in only one of two ways: through the Holy Spirit or by demonic means. The Bible warns us about seeking mediums and practicing sorcery (reference Leviticus 19:31, Deuteronomy 18:10-12, and Galatians 5:19-21), and Paul even casts out a spirit of divination from a slave girl in Acts 16:16—likely the very same type of spirit the mediums were invoking in the study.

Don't be deceived into thinking this is made up. The Bible recognizes the existence of these deceptive spirits. For example, 1 John 4:1 reads, "Beloved, do not believe every spirit, but test the spirits to see whether they are from God, for many false prophets have gone out into the world."

Interestingly, Dr. Newberg's study also compared the frontal lobe activity of these experienced mediums with that of novice mediums who were still learning to turn themselves over to a state of demonic possession. When both groups tried to channel spirits, the novice medium's frontal lobe activity was significantly different than that of the experienced mediums. The novice mediums' frontal lobe activity, in comparison, had just the opposite effect, with higher activity than the normal writing.

I encouraged Dr. Newberg to do a study comparing brain activity from people genuinely speaking in tongues with that of people making it up. Though this study has never been done before, I would imagine drastically different lobe activity similar to the comparison between experienced and novice mediums.

Dr. Newberg believes this to be the case as well. He explained that what happens to the brain when someone prays in tongues has a unique signature that has never happened before. Likewise, there is another unique signature when mediums successfully put themselves in a state of possession.

As a medical researcher, Dr. Newberg said that his studies couldn't prove or disprove what those involved in the study thought was happening. But what he could say was, "These types of spiritual experiences, speaking in tongues, and mystical experiences are profoundly real and have a tremendous impact on the people who have those experiences."

In terms of spiritual experiences and speaking in tongues, the existence of the demonic imitation (something the Bible clearly warns us about) shouldn't make us afraid of pursuing the truth—something the Bible tells us to earnestly desire.

Sometimes when I pray in tongues, God gives me ideas for my life, my ministry, and my business. Scripture, science, my own experience, and the spiritual evidence of countless others who pray in tongues have proven my friend's argument wrong. If Dr. Newberg's subjects, who sang in tongues, were making it up and were just engaging in random babbling, their frontal lobe should have blossomed with activity just like the monks. I can even do math in my head while praying in tongues; good luck trying to do multiplication for an extended period of time while making up random sounds.

IS THIS FOR ME?

Have you ever been challenged in what you believe? Maybe you're being challenged right now. If so, please don't close this book and walk away. Don't allow the enemy to offend you or make you angry. Offense and anger are not Fruits of the Spirit and do not come from God. Proverbs 4:23 admonishes us to guard our heart, but we also need to guard it in the manner Scripture says, in the context of when it was written.

This chapter is an invitation to go deeper with God. When we are challenged, we should go back to the Scriptures and make sure that we have been interpreting them correctly. I know pastors across denominational lines who pray in tongues and pastors from various denominations that actively teach against praying in tongues. I've seen this gift in operation among the poor in Haiti (which you will read about later), the persecuted in Vietnam, and from all walks of life in the United States. I know stay-at-home mothers, doctors, entrepreneurs, construction workers, university professors, and countless other Christians who pray in tongues daily. There are Christian millionaires and billionaires who use the practice of praying in tongues in their life every day.

THE "SPIRITUAL ADVISOR"

Maybe our favorite pastor, although a great theologian, has it wrong about speaking in tongues. One time after coming back from Haiti and seeing Haitians getting filled with the Holy Spirit with the evidence of speaking in tongues, I felt compelled to share the story with an entrepreneur I knew. He was hesitant about what I shared and said he wanted me to meet with his "spiritual advisor," who was a Baptist pastor, to talk about the topic. Many Baptists believe speaking in tongues ended with the death of Jesus' apostles. Talk about pressure!

I jumped on a Zoom meeting with them both, and before I shared my testimony about what God was doing in Haiti, the entrepreneur adamantly defended me to the "spiritual advisor." He let him know that I wasn't crazy and that I was legitimately doing my best to serve God. The entrepreneur recorded the conversation so he could have it as a reference for later. At the end of the conversation, the "spiritual advisor" told the entrepreneur that in regards to the Gifts of the Spirit and speaking in tongues, I had A++ theology! I have the recording of this, a recording that in the wrong hands could potentially get him kicked out of his fellowship!

The entrepreneur was astonished to hear his "spiritual advisor" vouch for everything I said.

"You don't understand how big of a deal this is," the entrepreneur explained to me. "He works closely with my pop (the entrepreneur's father). He's actually my pop's pastor, and my pop oversees all the Baptist churches in the region." The entrepreneur went on to say that for his "spiritual advisor," a close friend of his father and a Baptist pastor and Bible school professor himself, to admit my theology was A++ was a BIG deal. "My father has actively kicked missionaries off of the mission field and out of the Baptist church for speaking in tongues!" the entrepreneur emphasized.

Within a month of the conversation with the entrepreneur and his "spiritual advisor," the entrepreneur received his supernatural prayer language by himself while praying in his bathroom. The Scriptures I sent him, mixed with my testimony and that of his "spiritual advisor," led him to ask God on his own to receive his prayer language. I never prayed with him to receive his prayer language. You can receive your prayer language in the same way my entrepreneurial friend received his. If you would like your own copy of the Scriptures I sent to the entrepreneur, you can get them for free at WildExpectance.com/Scripture.

This conversation happened after the landmark rule reversal on the "spiritual embargo" placed on missionaries within the Baptist church (which prevented them from praying in tongues). There was a Washington Post article that helped shed additional light on this entitled, "Southern Baptists to open their ranks to missionaries who speak in tongues," which was published in 2015. The article states that between 2005 and 2015, praying in tongues was grounds for immediate dismissal by the Southern Baptist Convention. It was big news when this reversal was made.

This was a big enough deal that I remember reading about this while I was upstairs at my friend's house in Germany. The mission team I worked with at UCLA was in the middle of a three-country "Haiti Expo Tour" traveling across Europe. We were raising awareness about Haiti, selling local artisan goods, and raising money to invest in job creation and a scholarship program for the rural Haitian village we supported.

BREAKING THROUGH THE SPIRITUAL EMBARGO

A little over a decade before my conversation with the "spiritual advisor," Joe and a few students enrolled in a prominent Baptist school came to Los Angeles to work with a videographer. They planned to create some early footage for Save the Storks, do strategic planning for the ministry, and build one of the first websites for the ministry. Before this moment, "Save the Storks" was just a slogan on a shirt that we sold at music festivals, alongside countless other shirts. Joe invited me along with the students to a prayer conference that was taking place in downtown Los Angeles with the hopes of raising some money for our first mobile sonogram unit. Afterward, I got blamed by the students that everyone there became charismatic and began praying in tongues! I was the only charismatic person in our group, and they needed a scapegoat who could explain what happened.

"People were barking in the spirit, Bryan. BARKING IN THE SPIRIT! Explain how that's Biblical?!" one of the students urged.

"Hey, you guys invited me. Going to that conference wasn't my idea. Don't blame me for it," I responded. Joe stood up for me at that moment, and though he wasn't very charismatic himself, he had witnessed my faith in action.

I didn't see the whole barking thing that the student was complaining about (I've never seen that, actually), and honestly can't explain that, other than whoever he was referring to was likely weird long before they got saved or filled with the Holy Spirit. Everything seemed perfectly normal to me. Plus, I was raised in that kind of emotionally charged environment with people raising their hands in worship. People on their knees or people lying on the ground worshiping God wasn't their vibe. I was surprised that they would come to Los Angeles to attend a conference like that. This was the kind of conference I would go to instead. I don't think they went back to any of the other services. That Sunday, we all went to church together north of Los Angeles. This service was the exact opposite of the conference, with no one raising their hands during worship, and the experience had low energy.

As we were leaving, I noticed the church had copies of Francis Chan's book, *Crazy Love*, sitting on a counter near the front door. I heard great things about the book and knew that Francis Chan was a prominent evangelical pastor. I decided to purchase a copy from the lobby before walking to the car. Once we got back to the videographer's house, I learned that the reason they were selling *Crazy Love* at the church we attended was because Francis Chan helped start it. He was no longer a pastor there (unfortunately for us) because he had resigned and moved to Northern California to start a church-planting network. I wish I knew it was Francis Chan's church because I would have paid more attention and showed greater appreciation for the service. I have a lot of respect for Francis Chan and the selfless and generous life he lives.

Years later, I saw Francis Chan speak at a conference similar to the charismatic one that had frightened the students. I was excited; Francis Chan was one of the speakers, yet surprised, having visited the church he started. *Why would he be speaking at this conference?* I thought to myself. I had assumed he believed just as my Bible school friends did, and yet he was speaking at this high-profile charismatic conference. I later learned this was because something was changing inside of him. As he began to read the Scriptures from a more objective lens, Francis Chan realized that what he was taught in seminary might not be the whole truth—this evangelical was slowly becoming charismatic.

When writing his book on the Holy Spirit, Francis Chan even went back and talked to some of his professors about the topic of the gifts of the Holy Spirit and speaking in tongues. In an online interview, Francis Chan shares this conversation:

"Can you defend this Biblically?" Francis asked his professor.

"Well, not Biblically. There was not enough evidence, so I also looked at history, and it just seems like the gifts died in this period. And when you don't see it, so when I put that together..." the professor responded.

Francis clarified that it wasn't all the professors who responded this way, but just a couple. Francis was shocked by the response of some of his professors because as he was reading the Bible, the Scripture showed there was more than what was being taught in the classroom.

These Bible students who were taught by these seminary professors would eventually be pastors and missionaries of the next generation, teaching congregations around the world to believe something that wasn't true and not even Biblically backed.

As Francis was on this journey of discovering the truth regarding the Holy Spirit, he befriended some other people he could talk to about this; it wasn't willingly, but they happened to sit on a board together for a local non-profit that served the inner-city poor.

At first, Francis was skeptical of one of these pastors. Francis recalls the first time this charismatic pastor led a Bible study for the board. He was expecting it to be something like, "I had a dream last night, and here is what the angel said," but instead, this pastor opened up the Scriptures and went into the context of the Scriptures powerfully. He taught in a way Francis didn't expect, all while mixing it with a lifestyle that was Christ-like in character. It was this friendship that launched Francis into a whole different world of speaking opportunities that would eventually land him as one of the keynotes for this charismatic conference.

Two years after first visiting the church Francis Chan started, I received a random Facebook message from one of the Bible school students, who was now a missionary in Taiwan. This was when there was still a decade-long "spiritual embargo" on speaking in tongues within this missionaries' denomination.

His Facebook message read: "Hey Bryan! I'm studying the Holy Spirit right now, reading *Forgotten God* by Francis Chan. Anyways, I'd appreciate prayers that God would open the eyes of my heart and if I am missing it that like, He would reveal what I'm missing, ya know?"

This Taiwan missionary knew he could count on the good ol' charismatic *crazy faith* Bryan to talk about this topic. We had mutual mission respect for each other, and I was preparing to leave for my third mission trip to Haiti. I was probably the only person he knew who spoke in tongues and the most charismatic person our mutual friend Joe knew. I had sent the Taiwan missionary a book on speaking in tongues earlier that year, which he admitted he had never read. It was clear, however, that God was starting to speak with him about the Holy Spirit.

"You have skype available?" I responded.

"Yessir," he responded.

We jumped on a Skype video conference call, and I had a Bible study with him, likely in the same way this charismatic pastor went through Scripture with Francis Chan. I went Scripture by Scripture through what the Bible said about speaking in tongues and the Holy Spirit. I then asked him if he wanted to pray with me right there over the video conference to receive his private prayer language. To be honest, I had been a missionary for less than three years at this point and didn't even know if you could pray for someone over Skype to receive the Holy Spirit.

I hope this works, I secretly thought to myself. I wasn't sure if I would instead have to lay hands on him in person for him to receive his prayer language. After all, that's how Paul prayed for people in Acts 19:6. Thankfully, the Lord didn't leave me or this Taiwan missionary hanging.

As we began to pray together, the Taiwan missionary received his prayer language and prayed in tongues for the first time in his life. Remember, these were still the days of the "spiritual embargo" on speaking in tongues.

"I have to keep it down," he said after he received it. If they hear me in the room next door, I will get in trouble. It's true, according to the official stance of his mission board, if they found out about him praying like this, he would have gotten kicked off the mission field. I'm pleased to say that he is still serving as a missionary in Taiwan a decade later. He still serves out of the same building too, but now he is the missions director.

AN UNEXPECTED BACKFIRE

Let's return to what happened during my junior year of college when that negative campus pastor challenged my beliefs on speaking in tongues. I went back to Scripture, prayed about what he said, and through study, knew that he had it wrong. I then made a mental note of the church he represented in case I met anyone else from that denomination. I was going to go out of my way to talk about the Holy Spirit to other people from his denomination, knowing that they very likely have been taught the same distortion of Scripture as the negative pastor. I had a conviction in my heart: maybe a chance encounter with someone from this denomination would be their only chance to know the truth regarding speaking in tongues.

About a month after I prayed for the Taiwan mission, having just returned from Haiti, I flew to Illinois to meet up with Joe and join that summer's rock festival tour with Save the Storks. On the first night I arrived, I learned that one of the girls who was on tour with us was raised in that same denomination as the negative campus pastor. I soon learned she was leaving early in the morning because her mother was dying of cancer. Our tour schedule overlapped only a single night.

Because of my conversation with that negative campus pastor in college, I decided to engage her regarding speaking in tongues. *This might be her only opportunity to know the truth,* I thought to myself.

We started talking about spiritual matters, and she was interested in learning more about what the Bible said about the Holy Spirit and speaking in tongues. There was another coworker present who was dismissive of the topic. I knew that this coworker prayed in tongues, and I had expected her to back me up—instead, she was a distraction by continually trying to change the subject. I was thankful when she eventually left.

After going through the Scriptures on the topic, I asked my first coworker if she wanted to receive her prayer language. She was hesitant at first, but after seeing speaking in tongues visible throughout the Scriptures, she, too, was convinced that she hadn't been told the whole story. I later learned that God had already been dealing with her on this matter. She had seen that

Nightline episode with Dr. Newberg that I mentioned earlier in this chapter and thought maybe there was something to it, but she had never met anyone who was led to take the time and prove it to her through Scripture. What I did was important to her.

What I appreciated about her denomination is its love for the Bible. If you can prove it in Scripture, they will believe it. I recognized other people on our tour who didn't believe speaking in tongues still happened today would likely use this as an opportunity to mock it. Because of this, we went outside to pray away from the main group. As soon as we started praying, she immediately began praying in another language. Being confident, we went back inside and asked if anyone else wanted to receive their prayer language.

"Did you know about this?" she immediately asked her dismissive coworker.

"Yeah," she responded.

"Why didn't you tell me!?"

"I didn't want to make a big deal about it."

By not making a big deal about it, the dismissive coworker was preventing someone from receiving this wonderful gift. If I had

SHE WAS HESITANT AT FIRST, BUT AFTER SEEING SPEAKING IN TONGUES VISIBLE THROUGHOUT THE SCRIPTURES, SHE, TOO, WAS CONVINCED THAT SHE HADN'T BEEN TOLD THE WHOLE STORY.

had that same attitude, my original coworker might have never received her prayer language, which she said encouraged her greatly when her mother died later that year. The dismissive coworker was insecure and had never been fully taught the importance of praying in tongues. It was something she did but didn't truly know the value of, so she tried to avoid the topic altogether.

Coincidentally, I later learned that the original coworker's eighth great grandfather had helped start that same denomination when he came to America from England with his son, Benjamin Franklin—one of the founding fathers of the United States.

I believe these coincidental happenings will start compounding more in your life when you allow yourself to pray for God's perfect will in an unknown language. You would probably agree that the Apostle Paul was used greatly by God. Maybe we should do more of what Paul did if we want to have the same kind of impact he had. In 1 Corinthians 14:18, it reads, "I thank God that I speak in tongues more than all of you."

If you are still in doubt, here are some more examples:

"For one who speaks in a tongue speaks not to men but to God; for no one understands him, but he utters mysteries in the Spirit" (1 Corinthians 14:2).

"Likewise, the Spirit helps us in our weakness. For we do not know what to pray for as we ought, but the Spirit himself intercedes for us with groanings too deep for words. And he who searches hearts knows what is the mind of the Spirit because the Spirit intercedes for the saints according to the will of God" (Romans 8:26-27).

"But you, beloved, build yourselves up in your most holy faith and pray in the Holy Spirit" (Jude 1:20).

Unfortunately, a lot of believers are taught theology out of context. Those who do believe speaking in tongues is for today often get another aspect of it confused. Because of this, I am going to bring some clarification.

Some different examples of praying in tongues in the Bible are praying as a personal prayer language, corporate tongues, and tongues in the form of a language you do not know. God wants everyone to have a personal prayer language that they can use anytime: this is the individual believer praying out the perfect will of God. As I mentioned earlier, when the Bible references praying in the Spirit, it is talking about tongues as a personal prayer language. The Bible tells us to pray like this in Jude 1:20.

If you're interested in additional Scriptures to study on this topic, I want to reiterate that you can visit WildExpectance.com/Scripture to get a comprehensive Scriptures list on the Holy Spirit and praying in tongues. I recommend you save this to your phone so that you can easily access these whenever you like and use it as a reference when talking about this subject to others. I have this same list on my phone that I share with others before praying with them to get baptized in the Holy Spirit with the evidence of speaking in tongues.

One of the reasons we can confidently believe that praying in tongues is for everyone is because right after the early disciples received the baptism of the Holy Spirit, Peter immediately preached the boldest sermon ever preached by him. After the sermon, he had the first altar call.

And Peter said to them, "Repent and be baptized every one of you in the name of Jesus Christ for the forgiveness of your sins, and you will receive the gift of the Holy Spirit. For the promise is for you and for your children and for all who are far off, everyone whom the Lord our God calls to himself" (Acts 2:38-28).

This promise is for you and your children and all who are far over. *Everyone* whom the Lord our God calls, He calls to Himself. You are an *everyone*, so you can rest assured that this promise is for you. We know you can ask with confidence to receive this because of the promise Jesus made in Luke: "For everyone who asks receives, and the one who seeks finds, and to the one who knocks it will be opened. What father among you, if his son asks for a fish, will instead of a fish give him a serpent; or if he asks for an egg, will give him a scorpion? If you then, who are evil, know how to give good gifts to your children, how much more will the Heavenly Father give the Holy Spirit to those who ask him" (Luke 11:10-13).

This free gift is available to those who make Jesus Christ their Lord and Savior. When this is prayed, this Spirit of God comes and dwells in them. Afterward, they can pray for what is called the baptism of the Holy Spirit, where they receive their private prayer language. Some people receive this at salvation, but there are stories in the book of Acts where this was a separate experience.

If you have not yet accepted Jesus, here is your second opportunity in this book. You can receive both salvation and the baptism of the Holy Spirit at the same time. As you pray, you will deal with any unforgiveness you have against other people and repent of your unconfessed sins to God.

Pray this extended prayer now. Don't just read it and think about it in your mind, but confidently confess this prayer verbally over yourself:

"Father God, I believe You sent Your Son to live a perfect life and to die on the cross for my sins. I believe You raised Him from the dead

after three days and that through faith in Jesus, I can have eternal life. I repent for any sins I've ever committed, either known or unknown. I forgive anyone who has ever sinned against me. I accept Your Son, Jesus Christ, as my Lord and Savior. Thank You for saving me. I ask that You lead me into what I should do with my life.

I now ask Your Holy Spirit to come and dwell in me. I ask that You baptize me with the promised helper, the Holy Spirit, and give me the boldness the Apostles had in the book of Acts. I ask that You give me my supernatural prayer language to pray out Your perfect will. I know I will receive my prayer language because You promised that I would in the book of Luke. I am receiving this free gift by faith right now. Thank you for filling me in Jesus' name, amen."

Take a few moments to breathe in and breathe out. Let whatever comes bubbling up out of your spirit vocalize even if it doesn't make sense. Afterward, praise God for what He has done for you.

WHAT ABOUT AN INTERPRETATION

I remember the first time I was used in a corporate setting to interpret an unknown tongue. I was on a mission trip in Haiti with other missionaries and students I worked with at UCLA. Our mission team gathered together for a prayer meeting. A female missionary I work with began to utter a series of sentences in an unknown tongue. While we waited for her to finish, no one said anything. After she delivered the word in tongues, there was a pause, and the room remained silent. I then knew that I had the interpretation. I had a strong conviction that seemed to come from deep within my stomach. It's difficult to articulate, but I had an inner knowing that I was to step out and give the interpretation. Reflecting on what Sean Smith told me, I realized that I didn't have a full tissue—I had half a tissue. I knew I would be disobedient to God if I didn't step out and begin to speak the interpretation God started to reveal to me. As I began to speak out the first few words God had given me, it continued into a complete thought. Afterward, the pastor affirmed that what I shared was indeed a message from God. After that moment, God would go on to use me as an interpreter of tongues in different ministry settings such as Haiti, the United States, and Vietnam.

I find confidence to be used by the Holy Spirit like this through the words Jesus taught His disciples: "...do not be anxious how you are to speak or what you are to say, for what you are to say will be given to you in that hour. For it is not you who speak, but the Spirit of your Father speaking through you" (Matthew 10:19-20).

The type of tongues given in these examples is different from tongues as a personal prayer language. This type of tongue and the interpretation was at the will of God. It was not a direct translation but an interpretation of the meaning using my vernacular and mannerisms of what God wanted to say—I had to physically speak forth the interpretation God was giving to me.

Tongues as a personal prayer language are available to everyone. As mentioned earlier, practicing your prayer languages increases your sensitivity to God. This is especially true when He desires to use you in an interpretation of tongues like I just explained or in any other Gifts of the Spirit as outlined in 1 Corinthians 12.

In the book of Acts, the disciples prayed in tongues, and it was heard by others in their own dialect. At that moment, I don't know if the disciples had received knowledge and fluency in those languages or not. This is because I've heard stories of missionaries praying in tongues and others knowing what they were praying while the missionaries remained oblivious. The Bible also doesn't say that believers at Pentecost continued to travel and preach in those newly learned languages. I have, however, heard stories of this and suggest you read the captivating book, *A Voice in the Night* by Surprise Sithole, who learned multiple languages supernaturally.

The book of Acts continues to have people receiving their prayer language years after it was first documented. In Acts 19:1-16, there is evidence of people receiving their supernatural prayer language—still happening 20 years later. I encourage you to go back and reflect on this chapter from time to time as you continue to develop your spiritual maturity as a follower of Jesus.

CHAPTER 11

A MIRACLE ON BRUIN WALK

Our ministry held three outreach tables a week on Bruin Walk, the walkway that cuts through the center of UCLA. Bruin Walk was usually packed with students heading to class. This was where we met countless students over the years who we invited to our services and events. Our ministry had a signup sheet for student leaders, interns, and other staff members who wanted to help with these weekly outreach tables. Many times I helped with all three but was specifically in charge of the table on Thursday.

Sometimes I gathered those on my outreach team to pray and worship God beforehand. Our ministry rented a small office on the corner of UCLA's campus, which made it the perfect place for us to pray before heading to Bruin Walk.

Our ministry wanted to see God move on this campus with signs, wonders, and miracles. We wanted students to get saved through faith in Jesus, healed from any sickness, and delivered from demonic oppression and addiction. I had the boldness to actually believe this could happen in the lives of our students on campus. My mindset was that if I was going to do full-time ministry and give up everything to be at UCLA, promises like these from the Bible had better be true. After all, I didn't move out to Los Angeles to commit my life to a lie.

INCREASING MY PRAYER EXPECTANCE

I was challenged by a conference I once attended with Sean Smith. Sean was in town attending this conference to sharpen his leadership and prophetic gifting. One of the speakers shared from John 4:35, "Do you not say, 'There are yet four months', then comes the harvest? Look, I tell you, lift up your eyes and see that the fields are white for harvest."

The speaker then explained that everyone was "harvestable" now. He encouraged his listeners in attendance to put a demand on the Gifts of the Spirit. This pastor had a worldwide ministry with a track record of being used in words of knowledge, the prophetic, and other Gifts of the Spirit; he had equipped many others to do the same.

He explained that we must be willing to put our faith in action in order to be used in the Gifts of the Spirit. The purpose of the Gifts of the Spirit is to bring unsaved people to Jesus and to encourage the believers. They are not gifts to make us superior to others or badges that exemplify our holiness. They are tools to help us do our job here on Earth. We're called to bring people to Christ, disciple people in their faith, and encourage other believers.

God will not force us to use these gifts but will bestow them as He wills if we are open to being a vessel through which He can move. This speaker's teachings stretched my faith for a greater expectation of miracles in my ministry. He also reinforced my understanding of the relevancy of the Gifts of the Spirit in the context of evangelism. By putting a demand on the Gifts of the Spirit, you can lead someone to Christ who otherwise might not be receptive. This may come in the form of divine healing or having knowledge about someone that only God could reveal and knowing exactly how to interpret it.

It's important to note that just because God reveals something to you, that doesn't mean that you're supposed to share it. God may have revealed it so that you can know how to pray with someone or know what to say in order to draw them closer to Christ.

THE WOMEN AT THE WELL

Just before Jesus talked about the harvest to His disciples, He met a Samaritan woman at the well. Jesus operated in the Gifts of the Spirit, resulting in prophetic revelation regarding this woman. He told her things that only God could have revealed. As a result of this brief conversation, the Scripture in John 4:39 tells us that many people in the area believed in Jesus because of her testimony about their encounter.

Jesus operated in a prophetic anointing throughout His ministry that led more and more people to Him. A legitimate encounter with the living God will do a better job leading someone to Christ than an argument. As believers, we should have an expectation and willingness to be used like Jesus was used so that we can make a bigger impact. I want to reinforce what I wrote about in an earlier chapter regarding Jesus's claim that those who believe in Him will do greater works; these works can include being used in the area of the prophetic for the purpose of evangelism.

MIRACLE IN THE MIDDLE OF CAMPUS

One afternoon, I was on the UCLA campus and saw a girl coming down Bruin Walk with a crutch. I tried to hand her an invite card to our service, and she totally ignored me. Her response was not uncommon, as there were countless other student groups out there fighting for her attention. Many students would put their earbuds in and do their best to ignore everyone.

When I think about times of rejection, I'm reminded of a video that a UCLA Ph.D. student in our ministry talked about during a mission trip we were on together. The video was from Penn Jillette of the magician duo Penn & Teller. Though Penn is an atheist, he had some really thought-provoking and challenging thoughts regarding evangelism:

> *"I've always said that I don't respect people who don't proselytize. I don't respect that at all. If you believe that there's a heaven and a*

hell, and people could be going to hell or not getting eternal life, and you think that it's not really worth telling them this because it would make it socially awkward—and atheists who think people shouldn't proselytize and who say just leave me alone and keep your religion to yourself—how much do you have to hate somebody to not proselytize? How much do you have to hate somebody to believe everlasting life is possible and not tell them that?"

"I mean, if I believed, beyond the shadow of a doubt, that a truck was coming at you, and you didn't believe that truck was bearing down on you, there is a certain point where I tackle you. And this is more important than that."

A LEGITIMATE ENCOUNTER WITH THE LIVING GOD WILL DO A BETTER JOB LEADING SOMEONE TO CHRIST THAN AN ARGUMENT. AS BELIEVERS, WE SHOULD HAVE AN EXPECTATION AND WILLINGNESS TO BE USED LIKE JESUS WAS USED SO THAT WE CAN MAKE A BIGGER IMPACT.

It didn't matter if this girl with a crutch didn't want my invite card. I knew she needed it, whether she thought so or not. I knew our weekly service would help draw her closer to God. When you have a strong conviction and strong confidence in your faith, you will stop caring what others think about you.

This girl ignored me and kept walking past me, but I didn't pack up my things and leave campus just because I was rejected. I didn't allow insecurities and rejection to stop me from doing what I was sent to that campus to accomplish.

"Do you believe God can heal you?" I asked her as she continued walking past me, undeterred.

She then stopped and looked at me.

"Yes," she replied.

We were in the center of the UCLA campus, and she said that she believed that God could heal her. I hadn't seen this much faith in all of Israel! If you don't get that reference, go read Matthew 8:5-10. I later learned that she had just returned from studying abroad in France and was barely hanging on to her faith.

I immediately prayed for her and felt nothing. The clouds didn't open up; I didn't hear the audible voice of God telling me He was pleased, and I didn't hear an angelic choir. I was just being obedient because the Bible says to pray for people.

Even though I didn't feel a thing, within five minutes, she started jumping up and down and walked away pain-free, without her crutch. She came to our next service and later got up and testified how God had healed her during our encounter.

Also, she shared how over the past six months, she had been struggling with feeling isolated in her faith. The tendonitis in her knee was so rough that she could barely get out of bed. She publicly testified that when I prayed for her, she was healed.

I have prayed for countless people over the years on UCLA's campus. Sometimes there was an immediate improvement; sometimes, there was not. To be honest, usually, when I prayed, it didn't seem like much happened. But that didn't stop me from having faith and stepping out, even when it was inconvenient (I will write more on this later).

There are people around you that need you to care enough about them to pray for them. Some people will be receptive, and others will not be, but that doesn't mean

WHEN YOU HAVE A STRONG CONVICTION AND STRONG CONFIDENCE IN YOUR FAITH, YOU WILL STOP CARING WHAT OTHERS THINK ABOUT YOU.

you should stop planting seeds of prayer. After all, faith the size of a mustard seed can move a mountain—something regarded as immovable when Jesus first introduced the wild idea in Matthew 17:19-20.

It's our job to be obedient and to plant seeds. God desires to move through each one of us, not just pastors. However, we have to continually take chances, stepping out to do our part by praying for others.

A DEMAND ON OUR AUTHORITY

While I was attending that conference with Sean, it seemed that many of the attendees there were being used dynamically for God. It appeared as though they were being used in a much more powerful way than I was, and I wanted to figure out why. I had prayed for the girl with the crutch, but why wasn't I seeing more supernatural healings when I prayed for others? During one of the morning sessions, I learned why. The other attendees were being taught that powerless Christianity wasn't an option.

Another pastor, who was actually hosting the conference, made clear the expectation for every pastor and marketplace minister affiliated with his ministry network. I share some of those expectations below:

- There is an expectation that we are to be lovers of God, others, and Christ-like in character. Many times, people fall away from Christianity or are turned off by the things of the Spirit because others are not Christ-like in character. We need to make sure this is never us and that we maintain a Christ-like character.
- There is an expectation that we are continually filled with the Holy Spirit and to be people of God's presence. There was a recognition of the importance of continually praying in the Spirit and spending time with God. The pastor explained how the presence of God wasn't the icing on the cake; it *was* the cake.
- There is an expectation that you advance the Kingdom of God with signs and wonders following. There was a demand and expectation that signs and wonders followed each person there as validation for the Gospel message. The last verse in the book of Mark exemplified this clearly. Mark 16:20 reads, "And they went out and preached everywhere, while the Lord worked with them and confirmed the message by accompanying signs."

The pastor said that we weren't to just preach the Gospel of salvation, but the Gospel of the Kingdom. This includes salvation but also includes healings, provision, and God's guidance in our life. I want to clarify that the pastor did not promise a life free from struggle. Psalm 34:19 reads, "Many are the afflictions of the righteous, but the Lord delivers him out of them all."

We will face struggles, betrayals, spiritual attacks, and countless other situations. However, we are to actively battle them every day and not attribute demonic attacks and our bad decision-making to God. I'm reminded of what Sean learned from his mentor Mario Murillo, who taught him that the presence of problems does not mean the absence of Jesus. If this were true, the apostle Paul would never have written, "I can do all things through Christ who strengthens me," from a prison cell when he wrote Philippians. From prison, he wrote a book that continues to mock the powers of darkness every time a saint reads it and is encouraged. The pastor who hosted the conference shared some additional expectations:

> WE WILL FACE STRUGGLES, BETRAYALS, SPIRITUAL ATTACKS, AND COUNTLESS OTHER SITUATIONS. HOWEVER, WE ARE TO ACTIVELY BATTLE THEM EVERY DAY AND NOT ATTRIBUTE DEMONIC ATTACKS AND OUR BAD DECISION-MAKING TO GOD.

- Bring revival and reformation to every sphere that you come into. There should be an expectation to shift atmospheres. Regardless if people were in the ministry or the marketplace, there was an expectation that people would come to know the Lord and encounter His presence.
- A commitment to tithing and generosity. A lack of generosity hurts us, and those God wants to help through us. By trusting God with our finances, we can break free from cycles of greed. Generosity isn't an option; it's a command. God doesn't just want to bless us, but He wants to bless others through us. We are to be a river and not a dam in the area of finances. A good analogy I've heard regarding generosity is this: when we are a flowing faucet with our finances by constantly pouring out, our pipes will always be full.

It is impossible for a flowing faucet to have empty pipes. It's also impossible for them to freeze. The same is true with our finances when we are led by God in our generosity.

If we set our faith towards these expectations from the Bible, I believe our lives will be more fulfilled, and we will have a bigger impact than any of us could ever imagine.

CHAPTER 12

THE AMERICAN MUSIC AWARDS

"You're staying at the W Hotel, right?" I asked MC Hammer.
"Yeah," he responded.

"Can I catch a ride back with you? I live near there, and my ride has left already," I boldly asked.

I had no clue how I was going to get home. This was an era before Uber and Lyft. As a broke missionary, I was wondering how I was going to make my upcoming rent payment. How could I possibly afford the luxury of an overpriced cab from downtown Los Angeles back to my place?

It didn't matter that Hammer had just closed out the American Music Awards and was watched by tens of millions of people live from the Nokia theater. I needed a ride home, and I knew that he was staying at the W, a famous hotel across from UCLA. If I could at least make it there, maybe I could figure something out.

THE TRAVEL AGENT

It all started during my first year in Los Angeles when I was waiting to meet a student for coffee. I was at the Starbucks in Westwood near UCLA. I was sitting inside the coffee shop, located in a quaint area next to the Fox

Theater, one of the few cinemas that hosted red carpet movie premieres.

"Can I use this chair?" the man asked me.

"Take it," I responded.

"I don't need to take it. I'll sit right here."

"Sure, that's fine."

The coffee shop was packed, and I didn't mind if he sat at my small table for two. I no longer needed to save the chair. I had just gotten word that the student who I was supposed to be meeting needed to reschedule.

It wasn't a coincidence that I was there. I specifically remember having the thought that I was supposed to meet with this student off-campus at this Starbucks instead of the usual coffee spot near the student union. The idea of meeting him there came as a faint impression, so soft that I could have easily missed it.

Not too long afterward, the man sitting beside me started asking me what I did for work and if I was a student at UCLA. I explained that I worked with a campus ministry there and had just moved to Los Angeles from Missouri.

"I'm in town from New York for a few days," he responded. "Let me buy you dinner sometime this week and tell you more about my work."

A free meal sounded great. I was surviving on frozen pizzas and leftovers from our events. I liked the idea of a free meal, and maybe this stranger would become a financial supporter of mine. Later that week, I met him in the lobby of the W Hotel where he was staying, and we proceeded to drive into Beverly Hills to get dinner at The Cheesecake Factory.

He began to explain to me that he was a travel agent. He booked travel accommodations for famous music artists and began showing me tour book after tour book from different artists he'd worked with over the years. The list included Michael Jackson, Britney Spears, The Backstreet Boys, Shakira, and countless other musicians.

He explained that at the end of each tour, a book was released that included people who worked on it. He then showed me his name on each of them. Evidently, he'd been doing this kind of work for decades. He said he was a preferred vendor for many of these tour managers. I didn't even know people still used travel agents.

At first, I didn't understand why he was telling me all about his career—I didn't care. I was getting a free meal and a look inside the mainstream music industry. I later learned that he was trying to get a discount on a MacBook and hoped that I was a student who was willing to use the student special to get him a deal at the UCLA bookstore.

Instead of finding a student, he found an evangelist. He applauded the work I was doing for students on campus, and we became friends over time.

Coming back from a mission trip to Haiti, I once found myself at a layover in New York. The travel agent had just gotten surgery, and he said that I was the only person to visit him at the hospital. He seemed lonely and driven by his work.

He was a nice person who would reach out and buy me dinner whenever he would come to town. He was a nonreligious Jew, and I saw my father in him regarding his mannerisms and lack of spirituality. His similarities to my father gave me a strong conviction to share my faith with him. Maybe I would be the only person in his life that ever shared the Gospel with him. Our meetings sometimes led to opportunities to share my faith and inspirational stories of the work I was doing on campus and in Haiti. Mostly, however, he liked to talk about his business. Being a player in the hotel industry, he also claimed to have a close relationship with the Hilton family and mentioned he would spend Thanksgiving every year at their home.

He offered me a job opportunity one evening when we were meeting for dinner. He said, "I'm working on the upcoming Rhianna tour, and I need your help. Can you help me put together a spreadsheet of hotels and cities? I will pay you $50 an hour."

This was early 2010, and being uncultured in pop music, I embarrassingly admitted I had never heard of Rhianna. To give you some context to her popularity, she is one of the best-selling music artists of all time, having sold over 250 million albums. Regardless of who she was, $50 an hour sounded like a million bucks. I had never made that much before in my life.

It was spring when he made me this job offer. My savings from the summer had dwindled, and I had no clue how I was going to make my rent payment that month. The opportunity to make $50 an hour was an answer to my prayers! I graciously thanked him for the opportunity and said I would do whatever he needed.

I didn't own a laptop yet, so I explained that we would have to do this job out of my house, specifically my bedroom, where my desktop computer was stationed. My room was a mess, so I made sure I did an extreme cleaning of it and the rest of the house. There wasn't a single thing left on my normally cluttered 6-foot by 6-foot corner desk, which I used for my computer.

"Your house is just like I keep mine...spotless," he said, impressed.

He was the accountant type: very clean, organized, and a little awkward. I had tricked him into thinking I was a clean freak, but would I be able to deliver what he wanted? He needed me to outline Rhianna's complex 30-city summer tour taking place from June 28th through August 27th. I'd never done this type of work before, and handling details wasn't my strong point. It couldn't be that hard, right? I had made it this far, and I wasn't about to turn back.

The tour started off in Seattle with Rihanna staying at the Fairmont Olympic Hotel, followed by a 141-mile drive up to Vancouver, followed by Calgary. This trip was immediately followed by 21 hours back to the West Coast before slowly making her way east and finally ending at The Renaissance Hotel in Syracuse, New York. He sat behind me for hours, multiple days in a row, as I pulled in room rates, destination times, and countless other details as quickly as I could. I just hoped that my speed, accuracy, and formatting were up to par as I prepared countless pages of detailed travel plans.

This process took hours of tedious work, which meant a big payday and enough money to survive yet another month. Thankfully, he was very happy with the work I delivered. There were even talks of the possible opportunity of jumping on one of his client's tours during the summer. I already had experience touring music festivals, so I thought this might be an exciting new door that was opening.

I later learned that he didn't just book the hotels for famous tours; he booked the artists' travel accommodations for the Superbowl, Golden Globes, Dick Clark's New Year's Rockin' Eve, and the American Music Awards (or AMA's for short). Little did I know, this happenstance connection would soon land me on the red carpet and years of free VIP tickets to the AMAs (valued at $1,000 per pair).

When I think about this story, I'm reminded of 1 Corinthians 2:9, which I shared in the first chapter: "...What no eye has seen, nor ear heard, nor the heart of man imagined, what God has prepared for those who love him."

I could have missed this opportunity if I wasn't at the right place at the right time. God is constantly placing unique, exciting, and unexpected opportunities in front of those who have the audacity to believe.

Nothing is too hard for God, but as the saying goes, *it's difficult to move a parked car.* Many of God's children don't believe that He is capable or willing to open significant world-changing platforms for them; others believe God does this, but certainly not in their lives. Have you ever fallen prey to this lie?

It's easier to set your expectations low rather than have a radically optimistic faith. I'm sometimes criticized for being too optimistic or having "pipe dreams." People don't want to risk the emotional hurt of disappointment if their dreams or desires don't come to pass. So instead, they play it safe inside a mental storm shelter they built for themselves—safe from the world and its dangers.

> HE WAS THE ACCOUNTANT TYPE: VERY CLEAN, ORGANIZED, AND A LITTLE AWKWARD. I HAD TRICKED HIM INTO THINKING I WAS A CLEAN FREAK, BUT WOULD I BE ABLE TO DELIVER WHAT HE WANTED?

THE RED CARPET AND NOT SO CHANCE HAPPENINGS

One evening, a couple of years later, the travel agent told me he had just booked MC Hammer's hotel and that he would be closing out the AMAs that year in a surprise appearance. I remembered that Hammer was a Christian and a former pastor. Because of this, I was really looking forward to seeing the closing act.

My friend Jonathan picked me up from my apartment, and we headed downtown for the 2012 AMAs. Before I continue, it's important that you know how I met Jonathan and how he pertains to this story. I originally met him at a Bible study during my first year in Los Angeles. It was one of those connections God wanted to happen yet almost didn't.

Our friendship resulted from a bizarre series of events that took place two years earlier on a morning flight back to Springfield, Missouri. I was trying to get some sleep when the flight attendant announced that there was a problem. Evidently, one of the plane's engines had gone out. In all my years of travel, I had never heard of this!

We had to make an emergency landing in Las Vegas to switch planes. When the passengers finally boarded the new plane, I could no longer sleep, so I decided to talk with the girl next to me. If we had not had to switch planes, I would have never met her. She was moving away from California but invited me to a Bible study taking place in Studio City near Los Angeles. Expecting to make some more Christian friends, I decided to take her up on the invitation when I returned to Los Angeles. I drove my scooter up and down the vast hills of Los Angeles into the valley for this evening's Bible study (I've since wondered if God took down that plane and inconvenienced the entire crew just to get me there).

PEOPLE DON'T WANT TO RISK THE EMOTIONAL HURT OF DISAPPOINTMENT IF THEIR DREAMS OR DESIRES DON'T COME TO PASS. SO INSTEAD, THEY PLAY IT SAFE INSIDE A MENTAL STORM SHELTER THEY BUILT FOR THEMSELVES—SAFE FROM THE WORLD AND ITS DANGERS.

I attended this Bible study only once but met Jonathan (an aspiring actor) there. When he learned about my ministry at UCLA, he said their Bible study had just had a guest speaker who was also doing ministry on that campus: his name was Jaeson Ma, a rapper and entrepreneur turned campus pastor. Jaeson had also been mentored by Hammer for years. He was on the tail end of his campus ministry career, but Jaeson had one last performance scheduled.

Jonathan encouraged me to attend this event with him. Jaeson had a hit single that he recorded with Bruno Mars that surpassed over a million views on YouTube. After his performance, he shared his testimony. At one point toward the end of his service, he started operating in the Gifts of the Spirit, which I wrote about in chapter ten. Specifically, he was being used in the gift of prophecy and knowledge as referenced in 1 Corinthians 12:8-10. Jaeson knew things about the people he prayed over that only God could have revealed and then prophetically encouraged them about their future. God uses these gifts to encourage others and to soften people's hearts—a heart that may otherwise be unreceptive to the Gospel.

It seemed as if Jaeson had something that I didn't. I wanted to be used like this too. It would be nearly a year and a half later before I saw this same style of public ministry manifest through someone else—this time through Sean Smith.

At the end of Jaeson's service, Jonathan introduced me to him. It was a brief encounter. Jaeson was nice and gave me his book on church planting in the collegiate setting. He had planted 200 house churches around the world already. Later that evening, Jonathan gave me his cell phone number (though I never used it).

The first year I was given tickets to the American Music Awards, I decided to bring Jonathan with me to avoid causing jealousy amongst my campus ministry peers. The travel agent who gave me the tickets was getting surgery and was unable to attend. Because of this, after the show, I tried to convince the person in charge of the VIP after-party guest list to let Jonathan and myself in on his behalf. There were others guarding the entrance to the after-party, but he appeared to be the one in charge.

"Wait here," he said as he kept going in and out of the after-party.

He seemed skeptical of me at first. A lot of other people who wanted to go to the after-party didn't have tickets. He knew the travel agent and couldn't validate if I was making it up or not that the travel agent was getting surgery. Finally, as the night progressed, he decided to believe me and let us in.

The travel agent graciously gave me VIP tickets again the next year for the AMAs. I brought someone else with me that second year, but yet again, I didn't have tickets to get into the after-party. Security was even stricter than the previous year, and I was, unfortunately, unable to get in no matter how hard I tried.

It was another year later, and Jonathan was picking me up from my apartment. I was about to attend the AMAs for the third time, and I had just let Jonathan in on the secret finale.

Jonathan and I both hoped for an opportunity to meet Hammer, especially because Hammer used to be in ministry, and he was a longtime mentor to Jaeson. I respected Jaeson spiritually from the different interactions I had had with him, and that reflected in my views of Hammer. To be vulnerable, I think I was looking for affirmation for my ministry work because Hammer used to be a Pentecostal pastor. This desire for affirmation came from feeling unsupported by certain family and church members back home.

After I told Jonathan that Hammer was going to be performing and that I wanted to meet him, we spent the rest of our drive praying for this to happen. We prayed together in tongues that God would somehow get us tickets to the VIP after-party once again and that Hammer would be there.

When we arrived at the show, we were seated in the VIP section on the right side, about 50 seats from the front. I didn't see Hammer visible anywhere. He was likely backstage preparing. It's an interesting feeling sitting in a room full of some of the most famous people in the world. We could see celebrities sitting not too far from us, just like noticing familiar faces across the sanctuary on a Sunday morning.

During commercial breaks, the theater was a zoo. The television audience doesn't realize that everyone gets up and walks around, mingling amongst themselves. As commercials wrap up, there's an announcement and verbal countdown with people madly rushing back to their seats. Those who don't make it back are stuck standing in the back and waiting out of view from the cameras until the next commercial break.

There was security between the general seating and our VIP seating. Our tickets allowed us to come and go as we pleased, right down to the center stage where all the A-list artists and paparazzi were.

During one break while we were down there, Jonathan tapped Justin Bieber on his shoulder to get his attention and to congratulate Justin on his award.

"What are you doing!?" his bodyguard quickly yelled. Justin was already being mobbed by the paparazzi, and his bodyguard was responding accordingly. We didn't want to add any additional pressure on Justin, so we decided to return to our seats.

I knew Jonathan wanted to make it in Hollywood. I laughed and said that he just got the "Bieber blessing," similar to the woman with the issue of blood who touched Jesus' garment. Laughing and continuing to joke about this, I made up a ridiculous scenario around what Justin said to his security after Jonathan tapped his shoulder:

"Who touched me?"

"Everyone is touching you, Justin."

"No, I felt the anointing leave me!"

Transitioning to serious thought, I was encouraged that Justin would later give his life to the Lord and allow himself to be used in ministry. I was very proud of him.

When I sat back and thought about it, I realized that these celebrities were just normal people attending their award ceremony after years of hard work, similar to a ceremony non-celebrities might attend for their own achievements. It's kind of like when I won outstanding varsity wrestler of the year my senior year in high school—except the AMA's was televised and included performances between awards.

There is idolatry in our culture over celebrity status and stardom that needs to be broken. These are real people with real emotions. Whether or not these celebrities are living in God's best, each one has a calling in their life, just as non-celebrities do; they're not just punching bags for our social media accounts or a topic to gossip about. What if, instead of complaining about or idolizing these celebrities, we prayed for them? Not just in theory, but what if we actually prayed that they would have a revelation of who Jesus was and use their influence to impact the world for Christ?

Whether you like him or not, just look at the impact Kanye West made in 2019 when he had a radical conversion back to the Lord. His conversion resulted in him releasing his popular album titled "Jesus is King," which brought thousands of young people around the world to Jesus. His testimony opened a great bridge to talk about Christ to college students who were otherwise uninterested.

CHAPTER 13

VIP WITH MC HAMMER

The people sitting in front of us were clearly important.

When Jonathan and I returned to our seats after the commercial break, I noticed that some people in front of us were wearing lanyards with laminated badges that said "VIP." We just had glossy paper tickets, making our VIP tickets look like a joke compared to theirs. I began to pray in tongues under my breath. I sensed that I needed to speak with the person four seats to my left in the row in front of me. Maybe this was our ticket into the after-party. Being drawn to him wasn't an unusual experience because I learned this from doing ministry. Let me tell you how this is a common occurrence for me.

HOW TO CONNECT WITH STRANGERS FOR THE GOSPEL

I would often walk into the UCLA student union by myself, buy Chinese food, and then pray God would highlight a student I should eat with who was sitting alone. It wasn't an audible experience. Instead, I was drawn toward a specific person as I would quietly pray in tongues.

People love to talk about themselves. If you let people talk and ask them questions, you will be remembered as the best conversationalist they have ever met. Once seated, I would ask the student some basic questions, including their year, major, and what they wanted to do when they graduated.

"What is your spiritual background?" I would eventually ask. That is such an inoffensive yet effective question to turn any conversation toward God. You should underline that and remember it.

At this point, the student would have talked the entire time. For all they knew, I was a Zen Buddhist. Yet, at this point, their guard was down. Even if they had been offended by a Christian in the past, I would still be able to have a spiritual conversation with them. Their answer to my spiritual background question determined how I phrased things. It was always my goal to navigate the conversation towards an invite to an upcoming service or event.

"WHAT IS YOUR SPIRITUAL BACKGROUND?" I WOULD EVENTUALLY ASK. THAT IS SUCH AN INOFFENSIVE YET EFFECTIVE QUESTION TO TURN ANY CONVERSATION TOWARD GOD.

Before we finished eating, I would give them my phone number and ask them to call me if they couldn't find our meeting location. I would then ask the student to text me their full name. This request was so that I could add their contact information to my phone. My justification as to why they had to text me immediately was that I didn't typically answer unknown numbers. Although true, it was more so because I wanted to follow up with them later if they didn't come to our event.

And there you have it! That is an easy method to invite a total stranger to a church service or event and get their number to remind them about it, all without being considered weird. If you ever decide to incorporate this process into your outreaches, please only do so with the same gender so they don't think you're coming onto them. This technique very well could work for getting you a date, but that's not why I shared this ninja trick, so please use it appropriately.

I challenged a friend working alongside me in ministry to try this outreach strategy. As an introvert, this was the last thing he wanted to do. One afternoon, he forced himself to go to UCLA and sit next to a stranger for lunch. Just thinking about the idea made him super uncomfortable, but he knew this was the right thing to do.

Let's pause here. What uncomfortable things is God asking you to do? I encourage you to plunge ahead just like my friend.

Fighting his fear and insecurities, my friend asked a Chinese scholar if he could join him for lunch. The scholar agreed and even ended up coming to our event that evening. He later started attending our weekly services, eventually accepting Jesus as his Lord and Savior! The scholar was so impacted by our ministry that he flew to Shanghai when the team of missionaries that I worked with at UCLA traveled to China. The scholar spent multiple days with us, even sleeping at the apartment we rented.

The ripple effects of obedience are monumental and compound every time we say, "YES." Don't be afraid! You will see how it worked out for me as I take you back to the VIP Section at the 2012 American Music Awards.

MY TICKET IN

Looking at the person who God highlighted in the row ahead of me, I searched for an opportunity to start a conversation with his group without being intrusive. I decided to initiate some small talk with the person directly in front of me during one of the breaks. Maybe I could find a way to bridge the conversation with the person four seats to his left. The person directly in front of me eventually asked me where I was from.

"You're from Missouri?" he replied excitedly. "My friend's from Missouri!" Pointing to the person the Lord had already highlighted to me sitting four seats over.

He quickly introduced me to his friend.

"Where are you from?" I asked.

"Chesterfield, what about you?" he asked.

"Lake of the Ozarks."

His eyes lit up, immediately blurting out the name of a prominent bar. He explained how he loved to go down there to party.

"That was my first job!" I responded in astonishment. I was blown away by the unlikelihood of this conversation.

"Are you guys going to the after-party?" he asked.

"I'm not sure yet."

I was still trying to figure out if there was a way for us to get into the after-party. Jonathan said he might have a friend who was working there, but we hadn't heard back from her yet.

"Have you figured out if you're going to the after-party yet?" he asked again later that night.

"I'm still not sure."

When the show was almost over, he turned around again and looked at me.

"Look, if you don't have tickets, just let me know. I'm trying to help you out here, and I am not going to ask again."

"Okay, we don't have tickets, but we want to go."

"I wouldn't normally do this for a total stranger, let alone a plus one— but I'm going to hook my Missouri boy up. Take my number and call me when it's over."

They left shortly after, not even staying for the final performance.

Soon after they left, will.i.am, the founding and lead member of the hip-hop group, The Black Eyed Peas, walked onto the stage to introduce the closing act.

"Millions have uploaded videos on YouTube, but there's only one person who has 700 million views in just a couple of months...the Korean phenomenon, my homeboy, PSY!" will.i.am shouted as the lights dimmed and quickly began strobing.

PSY was performing his hit song "Gangnam Style," whose music video would go on to become YouTube's most-watched video by the end of 2014, surpassing 2.1 billion views. The number of views was so high that it required Google to "upgrade" YouTube's back end just to support it.

I was excited about this performance because this was a widely popular song among college students, resulting in our ministry performing a spoof on the video earlier that year. I didn't know PSY was a part of the closing act!

Midway through his performance, there was a pause, and the whole theater went dark. Out of the darkness came Hammer's booming voice.

"Stop! Hammer time!—"

"Oppan Gangnam Style."

"Too legit...too legit to quit—"

"—Gangnam Style."

"Too legit...too legit to quit—"

"—Gangnam Style."

Hammer, PSY, and their entourage of dancers performed a mixed rendition of "Too Legit to Quit" before transitioning back into Gangnam Style and doing PSY's famous gallop dance, in sync, as the whole crowd went nuts. You can actually find the clip of this online by searching for "PSY Hammer AMAs." It was absolutely incredible. You should take a break from reading and go watch that video now. It will make this chapter interactive, and you will have a greater appreciation for what happens next.

After the show, we began to make our way out of the auditorium and toward the Ritz Carlton ballroom, where the VIP after-party was taking place.

There was a mob of people also headed toward the Ritz Carlton. They had special tags on the bottom of their tickets that said "After-party," a tab we clearly did not have.

I called and began to text the person I had met at the show. He came out shortly through the layers of security to meet us.

"Follow me."

We began to confidently and quickly pass everyone else as he flashed his all-access credentials at each security checkpoint. He was boldly walking in as if he owned the place.

We walked into the main ballroom, where he quickly took us past another layer of security to another section of the ballroom. It turns out there wasn't just the VIP after-party. There was also the VIP section of the VIP after-party. He quickly introduced us to his boyfriend, who evidently was in charge of the entire event. The person who got us into the after-party came with the one person who was in charge of and ran the entire corporate VIP after-party for the AMAs!

"How long have you been together?" he asked.

"We're just friends," I promptly responded.

He falsely assumed that because I was at the AMAs with a guy instead of a girl, Jonathan and I were a couple. After we talked for a little bit, I decided to leave the VIP section and head to the dance floor. I didn't know if Hammer was even at this party. Many of the artists don't attend the corporate VIP after-party.

I might as well have some fun and boost my confidence, I thought to myself. If you ever get an opportunity to learn to breakdance, take it! It's the best physical exercise I've done since my wrestling years. I learned to breakdance my junior year in college, and that skill has yielded a great return in social settings. You never know when it might come in handy.

Unfortunately, there weren't a ton of people on the dance floor. It's not the corporate executive vibe, I guess. However, I noticed that one of the other people near me wore a lanyard that read "Hammer." I was getting close! Maybe my wild dream was about to become a reality.

"Where is Hammer at?" I asked.

He then pointed to the corner in the VIP section. *I just came from that area,* I thought. I decided to continue to embrace my hip hop skills next to whom I eventually learned was Hammer's son.

Finally, I saw Hammer approach the dance floor. This was my opportunity. *Play it cool, play it cool,* I thought to myself as I continued to pray in tongues under my breath. "God has brought me this far. Here's my chance. Don't mess this up."

I knew Hammer liked Jaeson. Jaeson used to do the job that I did at the time. In that line of thinking, that meant he liked me. That's a good ice breaker, right? I'm sure it's a better connecting point than anyone else had in here. There had to be a spiritual connection between us. After all, nearly thirty years earlier, he was in a rap ministry called "Holy Ghost Boys." Surely, this former Pentecostal preacher would appreciate the work I was doing for the Kingdom of God.

"Hi...I do campus ministry at UCLA. Do you know Jaeson Ma?" I quickly asked him.

I didn't have a plan after that! Was he going to say, "That's cool," and then just walk off? If so, that would have been an underwhelming end to the evening. But everything was happening so fast, and there was so much excitement in the room; that couldn't be the end of our brief encounter. Why was I even trying to get ministry affirmation from this celebrity?

He immediately looked at me, and his countenance changed.

"Yeah, he's like family," he answered, surprised.

Then he immediately reached into his pocket and pulled out his phone.

"Look, he's calling me now. Here, you take it."

Then Hammer handed me his cell phone.

Wow. He just handed me his cell phone after closing out the show with PSY and was just watched live by millions upon millions of people just a couple of hours earlier. This is crazy! Not only did I just meet him, but he handed me his cell phone!

"Hi Jaeson, this is Bryan Citrin," I said as I ran out of the ballroom so that I could hear him.

I'm imagining what this looks like, taking his phone and immediately darting out of the room.

"Where are you guys at?" Jaeson asked.

"We're in the Ritz Carlton Diamond Ballroom D," I replied.

"We will be there soon."

The thought "text him from your phone" went through my mind as I hung up. I suddenly remembered Jonathan had given me Jaeson's number a couple of years earlier. Remember, the voice of God can come as a sudden awareness, followed by a unique conviction.

I didn't know if that was even Jaeson's number anymore as I pulled out my phone to look for his name. I texted the information that I had just told Jaeson anyway as I walked back into the ballroom and over to Hammer.

"He is on his way," I told Hammer.

Moments later, Jaeson texted me back. It was his number, and he started communicating with me now instead of Hammer.

"They aren't letting us through," Jaeson texted.

"Where are you at?"

"We're at the entrance area for the after-party."

"They aren't letting him in," I told Hammer.

"Take me to him," he commanded.

From that moment on, I became part of the entourage. I led Hammer and his crew out of the party and down the hall. Hammer would hand me the camera to take photos of the people who would stop us as we made our way down through security to the entrance of the after-party.

Jaeson brought someone with him and quickly introduced him as a friend from Justin Beiber's agency.

As we all got into the elevator together, Jaeson didn't ask me why I was at the after-party. He didn't ask me why I was hanging out with his mentor. He didn't ask me how I got tickets to the award show.

We briefly spoke, and I said I was still doing ministry at UCLA. He was surprised that I was still doing ministry there. As we approached the first layer of security, they refused to let us back in.

"This is my party!" Hammer insisted to the security guards.

They didn't recognize who he was, and none of us had entry badges. After arguing back and forth, they soon realized that they had made a big mistake.

"We're so sorry!" they said as they let us back in.

Upon reentering the ballroom, Jaeson saw that my friend Jonathan was there. They originally knew each other in 2006 when Jonathan was a student at the University of California, San Diego. Jaeson was there doing campus ministry before transitioning his focus to UCLA and countless other places around the world. They would always run into each other at the most random places. For example, he didn't expect to see Jonathan at the actor's Bible study, at which he was guest speaker for years later in Los Angeles. They were both shocked to see each other, yet not surprised.

Jaeson came out to support his longtime mentor and reconnect with him. He was also ecstatic to be there for the breakthrough of Asian culture in American Hollywood Media. As a proponent for more Asian diversity in Hollywood, it meant the world to see his longtime mentor close out one of the top media events of the year with the South Korean sensation, PSY.

There was no way I was about to leave the party early, but Jonathan was my ride. As the night slowly grew later and later, Jonathan said he needed to take off. I told him he could leave without me. I had no clue how I was going to get home—staying at the party was purely a faith-based move. All I knew was that I was hanging out with Hammer and his crew at the after-party, and I didn't want to squander this experience.

Uber and Lyft hadn't been invented yet. I knew that cabs were overpriced and that I didn't have the money for one anyway. As a broke missionary, I had to figure out a different way back to my apartment. All I had was a $100 bill that was just given to me for my birthday a week and a half earlier. That may seem like a lot, but my bank account was nearly empty. I had to find the money for groceries, rent, utilities, my phone bill, the minimum payment on my credit card; the list goes on. Things were so tight that I had put my student loans on forbearance because I couldn't afford the small minimum payment each month. As I reflected on how I was going to get home, I decided I would let God solve this problem. He had already brought me this far.

As the night wrapped up, more and more people began to head home. Hammer, Jaeson, and his crew started making their way out of the party, down the escalator, and toward the parking garage. I joined them.

Hammer's entourage was slowly fading away, and now we were in the parking garage. Jaeson said his farewells. I was still trying to figure out how I was going to get home. Finally, it was just Hammer, his driver, his son, his bodyguard, and me.

What would you have done if you were there? It's easy to let our pride, fear, and ego keep us trapped in a bad situation. At that moment, I was walking home unless I humbled myself and asked for help. And even if I asked, I still might be walking home if God didn't intervene. This was my only shot, so I went for it.

"You're staying at the W Hotel, right?" I asked Hammer.

"Yeah," he responded, not asking me how I knew that.

All I knew was that my ride had left, I was broke, and that I had to figure out how to get home, however the means. Famous or not, I knew Hammer was headed to my area.

"Can I catch a ride back with you? I live near there, and my ride has left already." I boldly asked.

"Sure," he generously responded.

"PRAISE GOD!" I'm yelled in my mind. "The Lord hath provided!" I had no clue what I was going to do otherwise. I felt as if I needed to go Old Testament-style when I got home and sacrifice an animal in gratitude! But seriously, He didn't leave me hanging in downtown Los Angeles at midnight, less than two miles from Skid Row. Thank You, God, and thank you, Hammer!

I got into the backseat of Hammer's Escalade, and we started making our way toward the hotel. To think, at the beginning of the night, I was praying in tongues for the opportunity to get into the after-party and to meet Hammer, who was closing out the show. Now, I was sitting in his backseat getting a ride home!

IT'S EASY TO LET OUR PRIDE, FEAR, AND EGO KEEP US TRAPPED IN A BAD SITUATION. AT THAT MOMENT, I WAS WALKING HOME UNLESS I HUMBLED MYSELF AND ASKED FOR HELP.

I know he was exhausted from an intense night, so I didn't dare bother him. He sat diagonally from me, scrolling through Facebook and unwinding after finishing his most important performance in years.

I wasn't about to be the annoying guy in the vehicle. I kept quiet, grateful I wasn't walking home. My next problem was figuring out how I was going to get from the W Hotel to my apartment. Catching this ride got me closer, but I wasn't home just yet. I felt way more comfortable being stranded in Westwood across from UCLA than downtown.

Once we arrived at the front of his hotel, I handed Hammer the second edition of my prayer magnet and thanked him for the ride. The magnet was a photo of me at UCLA. It was better than my first edition, which had a photo of me in front of the ocean that read, "Please pray for Bryan." My friends joked that the original prayer magnet made it sound like I was dying of cancer or something. It also invoked jealousy and made it look like people were praying for me to hang out at the beach all day. So, I changed it to a photo of me on the campus.

I've given out countless prayer magnets over the years to people at Christian music festivals across the nation. Missionaries need to know how to market themselves and stay top of mind. The prayer magnet is perfect for this. Once it's put on someone's fridge, it usually stays there. I've heard stories of people continuing to pray for me years later because they would see my face every time they were hungry. Who knows, Hammer might even have it on his fridge! Ignorance is bliss, and so I'll keep thinking that. It's infinitely more likely though that he lost it or threw it away.

After I handed Hammer my prayer magnet, he told me to be blessed with my ministry and told his driver to take me wherever I needed to go. The Lord had provided yet again!

As I rode back to my hot, un-airconditioned, one-bedroom apartment, I reflected on what had just happened. At the after-party, they had all-you-could-drink liquor and various other drinks. Everything was free, and because I don't drink, I took advantage of the after-party's endless supply of Red Bull energy drinks. This meant that I couldn't sleep.

All the excitement made me hungry, so I decided to go on a prayer walk, heading down the street toward a late-night taco truck.

THE PEAK OF A WILD NIGHT

I lived less than a five-minute drive from Beverly Hills. I would soon learn that a five-minute walk in the other direction would lead me through a rundown and dangerous neighborhood. I lived on the edge of both these extremes.

This rough area was the only thing standing between my apartment and my late-night taco truck. It wasn't until my friends told me I was crazy the next evening that I truly understood my stupidity. It was risky to walk around that area at night by myself. I could have been mugged or worse. I was newer to the area and didn't know any better at the time.

As I walked and prayed in tongues, reflecting on everything God had just done for me, I passed someone. He seemed normal, though also mindlessly wandering around in the middle of the night. After I got about 10 feet past him, I sensed that God wanted me to help him financially.

No, not the $100 in my wallet! I need that! I thought to myself. This wasn't money I had budgeted for a cab and certainly wasn't money I had available to give to a random stranger who might use it for drugs.

Did my ignorance of how dangerous it was to walk in that area at night position me to help this person? I stopped and turned back to ask him how he was doing financially.

"I'm doing fine," he responded.

Okay, he doesn't need my help, I thought. *I just dodged a bullet. The idea that this perfectly normal, non-homeless looking person needs help must be completely in my head.*

But what if it wasn't? I didn't want to take that risk. I pulled out my wallet and took out the crisp $100 bill, and looked at it. I still sensed that God wanted me to give it to him. Giving him that money hurt like giving away thousands of dollars—I was yet again the widow giving my mite. After I handed it over, he immediately started breaking down emotionally. I didn't know his story or situation, but there was clearly a significant need in his life.

After giving him the money, he was open for me to share my faith with him and about what God had just done for me at the AMAs. He used to believe in Jesus but now had doubts regarding his faith. He wasn't sure if faith in Jesus was the only way to Heaven. I ended up praying with him to rededicate his life to the Lord and for him to accept that Jesus was the only way to salvation.

I then asked him if he wanted to receive the baptism of the Holy Spirit. I explained what that meant and how he would receive a supernatural prayer language. He said he wanted this, and as I began to pray with him, he instantly started praying in tongues with me. After we prayed, I gave him my prayer magnet and said he could reach out to me with any questions about what had just happened.

We parted ways, and I continued to walk toward the taco truck again, reflecting even more intently on the evening. This night kept getting crazier, and I was overwhelmed with emotion.

Moments later, I sensed the Lord speak clearly to me. "That was nothing," referencing all the steps it took to get into the AMAs, the after-party, meeting Hammer, the perfect timing of everything, and Hammer driving me home.

"But *that*, that was something," referencing this stranger rededicating his life to the Lord and getting baptized in the Holy Spirit.

I reflected again on what God said: "That was nothing...but *that*, that was something."

Those words changed my life. All 20 of these things had to line up perfectly for me to get a ride home from Hammer:

1. I had to have tickets to the award show.
2. I had to know that Hammer was closing out the show.
3. I had to sit right behind the group whose friend planned out the after-party.
4. I had to know which person to talk to in that group.
5. I had to be from Missouri and have worked at this person's favorite bar in my hometown.
6. He had to get both Jonathan and me into the after-party.
7. Hammer had to attend that party.
8. I had to head to the dance floor when I did and know how to breakdance.
9. Hammer had to come to an area where I could easily approach him.
10. I had to know his friend Jaeson and that Jaeson did ministry at UCLA.
11. I had to talk with Hammer at the exact moment Jaeson called him.
12. I had to have Jaeson's number saved on my phone so that I could text him.
13. I had to have faith to let my ride leave without me.
14. I had to know that Hammer was staying at the W Hotel.
15. The W Hotel had to be near my home.
16. I had to have the opportunity to walk with Hammer to his car.
17. I had to have the boldness to ask Hammer if he was staying at the W Hotel.
18. I had to have the guts to ask Hammer for a ride home.
19. Hammer had to have the compassion to say "yes."
20. I had to have enough favor for Hammer to ask his driver to take me all the way home.

And yet, all those improbabilities—and as some might say, impossibilities—were nothing in God's eyes. This was easy for Him to orchestrate. The most important thing to God that evening was that this stranger, in the hood, in the middle of the night, would receive unexpected provision, rededicate his life to Jesus, and get baptized in the Holy Spirit with the evidence of speaking in other tongues.

God wants to do incredible things for us and through us, but we have to have faith, a willingness to step out into the unknown, and be obedient to how He wants us to do it.

As I mentioned earlier, 1 Corinthians 14:2 says, "For one who speaks in a tongue speaks not to men but to God; for no one understands him, but he utters mysteries in the Spirit."

In other words, this Scripture says that when we pray in tongues, we pray mysteries in the Spirit. Our past is not a mystery; our present is not a mystery, but it's our future that's a mystery. We can pray out divine appointments not only for our lives but intercede for others when we pray this way.

Praying in tongues as a personal prayer language is something I practice every day. It's this aspect of my prayer life that has given me the sensitivity to the Lord to walk into experiences like this. This valuable tool has helped my ministry, my business, and my relationships grow. It's the body of Christ's best-kept secret to equip us with boldness and power to fulfill our destiny. Praying like this starts the process of setting up these God-moments that He wants for our future.

I had to continually be at the right place, at the right time, for everything to have played out the way it did. I had to be fully sensitive to God's guidance. Even before arriving at the AMAs, Jonathan and I spent time praying together in tongues about our prayer requests for the evening. Throughout the night, I continued to pray in tongues at various times under my breath. The results? An incredible story, ending with a finale that trumped the entire evening! I want to reinforce that this supernatural and personal prayer language is something that God desires for you to have as well.

CHAPTER 14

BREADCRUMBS
OF FAITH

"I really want to help you, but the Lord told me not to," the businessman told me.

I knew that his wife was a successful dentist with three practices. I was grateful that he was allowing me to share a hotel with him for free during the conference that we were attending. I had hoped he would be more enthusiastic about helping with my mission work, but instead, he shared how he wanted to, but God wouldn't let him.

It felt as if the Lord was going behind my back and talking bad about me. How was I supposed to survive in missions if the Lord was actively working against me? How would you have felt in that situation?

The businessman's words brought me to one of my lowest points emotionally in ministry. I was struggling to pay my bills every month, I had maxed out a credit card, and I desperately needed a vehicle.

In light of all my sacrifices to you, this is how you treat me? I thought to myself. I was beginning to question if I missed it; was I really called to move out to Los Angeles to be a missionary?

The businessman and I had just finished lunch, and it felt as if all Hell had broken loose against my emotions. What was I to do? We were attending a Christian conference together in Tulsa and made our way to the service as I fought feelings of doubt, rejection, and insecurity.

When we walked into the building, I saw someone who was briefly introduced to me the day before at our hotel. I didn't really know this person, but he walked up to me when I needed it the most and said, "The Lord wanted me to tell you that He is aware of your situation, and He has taken care of your request."

Have you ever been in a moment where you needed to hear from God? What if this stranger wasn't obedient in sharing this message with me at that crucial moment? When he shared this with me, all the hopelessness and doubt that I was feeling left my body. I immediately felt peace overtake me. I desperately needed this Word from the Lord right then and am so glad that he was obedient.

IT FELT AS IF THE LORD WAS GOING BEHIND MY BACK AND TALKING BAD ABOUT ME. HOW WAS I SUPPOSED TO SURVIVE IN MISSIONS IF THE LORD WAS ACTIVELY WORKING AGAINST ME?

Whatever you're going through today, I say the same thing to you: the Lord is aware of YOUR situation and has taken care of your request. When this stranger shared that message with me, it suddenly gave me the strength that I needed, and a *wild expectance* from God rose up in me.

"You said You'd provide, and it doesn't matter how I feel," I declared. "I am not led by my feelings, and I am not led by fear; I am led by peace. Thank You, Lord, for taking care of my request."

At that moment, I became even bolder. I wanted to make sure God actually knew my problems, so I laid it out for Him saying, "If You're so aware of it, let me tell You what I need. I need money for Haiti, I need a new car, and I need $10,000!"

I then thanked God for these things that I needed in advance. Keith Moore once said that his most powerful series was 'Thanksgiving Victory.' He preached about the importance of expressing your faith by thanking God before you ever see the physical manifestation of your prayer request. "If you believe that God has answered your prayer, then you are to thank Him afterward, knowing you have received it," he said.

I then thanked God that He would give me an opportunity to share details about my mission work at a church I believed He wanted me to attend on Sunday. Chip Brim had given me an opportunity to share at his conference in Las Vegas earlier in the year, and we briefly discussed the possibility of speaking at his church in Oklahoma.

During a time of prayer some months earlier, I put on my calendar when I thought I could make it into town from Los Angeles to speak at his church. The problem was that I couldn't reach him to confirm the date.

The events leading up to this moment were like following faint breadcrumbs from the Lord. I didn't have the name of his church! How was I supposed to speak somewhere if I didn't know what it was called or where it was? All I knew was that his church was in the Tulsa area. In hindsight, I don't know why I didn't just search for the church online. It's easy; just put the pastor's name and the town he's from into the search engine and press enter. I just did a Google search right now, and his church came up as number two. Maybe God had clouded such an obvious solution in my mind because He didn't want to lose any of the glory for what was about to take place.

A week earlier, I was in Springfield, Missouri, trying to schedule meetings with different people to make an appeal for them to support my mission work. For whatever reason, no one was available on Saturday. I later learned that my pastor was going to be in Branson, Missouri, at a conference put on by Chip's mother, Billye Brim.

I thought that maybe God was leading me to go to this conference so that I could reach Chip. Thankfully, I was able to speak with his mother afterward. She explained to me that I needed to speak with her son's wife if I was to get in touch with him and graciously gave me her number.

When I finally reached Chip's wife, she wasn't sure I would be able to share that Sunday because the church typically needed a heads up for any guest speakers.

I've been trying to get in touch with your husband for months! I thought to myself. God said He was aware of my situation; I believed God that I could speak at this church. I decided to show up in faith that Sunday to see what played out. Failure wasn't an option. I was getting ready to leave for Haiti, and I didn't have the money to go. If Chip let me speak, maybe the church would take up an offering for me to help cover my Haiti mission trip.

When I arrived, Chip was explaining how they had just held a youth conference and had seen great results regarding teenagers deepening their faith in Christ. I couldn't have come on a better Sunday. I used to attend that conference when I was in high school. This conference made a significant difference in my life. It was at that conference when Chip prayed for me as a teenager to receive the baptism of the Holy Spirit with the evidence of speaking in tongues.

Now, years after this experience, I was at his church on the Sunday after his annual youth conference. I was a powerful, living testimony of the fruit that resulted from the seeds he sowed nearly a decade before. It was the perfect testimony to go along with his sermon. Because of this, he graciously invited me forward and allowed me to share details about my mission work. I proceeded to share some testimonies of what God was doing on the UCLA campus, as well as the need for what we were doing in Haiti.

They graciously received an offering that covered the amount of money I needed to raise for my mission trip to Haiti. God had answered my first prayer from the situation He said He took care of earlier that week!

Not too long after, I received an email from the church. Someone who watched the online recording of me was interested in mailing me support directly. I sent her my address in the following email:

> *Hey* ▮▮▮▮▮▮▮▮ *,*
>
> *I hope you are having a wonderful afternoon.* ▮▮▮▮▮▮▮▮ *forwarded me your email, and I would like to thank you for your interest in partnering with my ministry. If you are free to give me a call, you can reach me on my cell phone at* ▮▮▮▮▮▮▮▮*, and I can tell you how you can support me directly as well as share about my recent Haiti trip. I just landed back in the states last week, and the trip went great.*
>
> *All direct support can be mailed to:*

Bryan Citrin

████████████████

Los Angeles, CA 90034

If you wish to receive a tax credit for the donation, there is another address I can give you that will allow for that. I can also mail you a form if you wish to become a monthly partner.

Thanks so much, and I look forward to hearing back soon.

I never received a response. There had been numerous people over the years who had expressed an interest in helping my mission work but didn't follow through. Because of this, I disregarded it in my mind.

Have you ever promised somebody something but didn't follow through? It happens to all of us. When considering helping a church, ministry, or missionary, my encouragement to you is to not get their hopes up by saying that you're going to help them and then forget. Do your best to follow through, and let your "yes" be "yes."

If something unexpected happens and you can't fulfill your promise, that's okay. Just let them know. They will be grateful that you notified them, as this allows them to better budget that loss. They may have been counting on your support to cover the cost of a ministry event, an upcoming trip, or maybe their rent.

Two weeks later, I received this unexpected letter in the mail:

Dear Bryan,

I enjoyed hearing your testimony when you were at ███████████████. *God had put it on my heart to get ready to plant a seed. I believe in many things and am standing in faith for many things. When He put it on my heart to plant a seed, I had no idea where He would lead me.*

While I was listening to the download of ███████████ *and you began to speak, our Heavenly Father said that you are the one. It is so amazing to me how He works. He began to speak to me about some of the things that I am believing for. One of them is my oldest son. He is just a little younger than you are. I am believing for God to get a hold of his heart and give him direction, and provide for his needs. It is my desire that he seeks God as his source. It would be very easy for me to give him this money to make things easy for him, but it is my desire that he looks to God and not me. So, I am sowing this seed to you to be a blessing to you and to acknowledge that I know that our Heavenly Father will take care of my son. I trust Him.*

The second thing that He spoke to me about is the fact that His children shall never lack. When we are obedient to Him, He provides everything we need. We do not work for Him for nothing. He is a Father who blesses us abundantly when we obey. I do not believe that you should ever lack for any good thing. When non-believers see us, they should see blessing and favor. They should want what we have…a Father who is a cup-overflowing God.

Continue to follow after Him. Continue to seek Him every second. Continue to do your part in the body of Christ, and we will do valiantly. His glory will flow through you, His Spirit and power will flow through you, and people's lives will be changed forever to the glory of God.

We are blessed to be a blessing!

Thank you for your obedience to the work of the Kingdom.

Jesus is Lord!

Your Partner in Christ,

Included in this letter was a check made out to my name for $10,000! God had answered my second big prayer through this offering!

When I returned from my trip to Haiti, I sensed that God wanted me to have a booth at Lifest, a Christian Rock Festival near Oshkosh, Wisconsin, put on by Bob Lenz. I knew I was supposed to be at this festival and booked a vendor slot in faith, but I didn't know how I was going to get there. I had a flight scheduled from Haiti to St. Louis with a layover in Chicago.

It turned out that Joe's family was on their way from the Chicago area to Lifest at the exact moment of my layover, so I was able to get off before my connecting flight and ride with them. Joe was there, too, with a booth for Save the Storks. He negotiated for us to stay at Bob Lenz's cabin while we were there. Bob was the head of the festival, so this was a pretty cool experience.

This was my first time having a booth at a festival since I had met Joe. This time, I was strategically across from him in the back of the vendor area. Normally, we would have been working together. However, I believed God wanted me to have a separate booth at this festival to sell Haitian paintings and bracelets. I had the creative idea of taking hand-painted Haitian canvases, cutting them into strips and turning them into snap-on bracelets. This idea sounded great in theory, but in application, no one really wanted these. I received the idea from another ministry that created custom bracelets from thread that made a killing at this festival.

I was discouraged because I couldn't sell my bracelets. I decided to stop caring about making money and instead would just pray for people at my booth. I had the opportunity to pray for multiple people to receive the baptism of the Holy Spirit. My friend was surprised that we could talk to a total stranger, share some Scriptures about the Holy Spirit, and then pray for them to receive their prayer language. He thought you had to wait for the mega evangelist to come into town to pray for someone to receive their prayer language. If we are supposed to pray for our friends and family members to receive Christ, why is it that we have to wait for them to get filled with the Holy Spirit?

During that festival, Joe graciously introduced me to a couple who were significant donors to Save the Storks. Little did I know that this generous Baptist couple would be a critical driving force in my mission effort.

My attendance at this festival was entirely God orchestrated. I, unfortunately, was not gifted in the area of administration and wasn't sure how I was going to get back to Missouri. Conveniently, a friend of mine from college was also at the festival. I had introduced him to Joe a year earlier, and they went into business together. Joe convinced my friend that he should also get a booth at this festival, specifically for the business in which they were both partners. It was this friend who eventually got me into digital marketing. He lived in Springfield, Missouri, so I was able to catch a ride back with him after the festival. Reflecting back on stories like this, I see how God really has helped me logistically, despite my lack of planning.

Within a month and a half of attending Lifest, I was able to explain my ministry needs to the couple Joe introduced me to. I explained the need for me to get a vehicle for my ministry.

"What type of car do you want?" they asked.

"I'm trusting God for a Ford Escape," I responded.

After I shared my need with them, God placed it in their heart to help me. This generous couple purchased me a Ford Escape that was only one year old with just 17,000 miles! They even paid to have it driven from Texas to Los Angeles. The driver they hired showed up at my apartment with the vehicle and asked me to drive him to the airport. He even bought me dinner. To top it off, they sent me the money to pay the registration taxes on this $15,000 vehicle.

God had provided all three of my big needs within 45 days of that prophetic promise!

The Lord provided for me in ways that I couldn't fathom! Reflecting back on my perception of God, God WAS talking about me behind my back. But he wasn't saying the kinds of mean things I originally perceived. Sure, He told my friend not to help me; but He only did that because He was telling Chip to let me speak; He was telling this concerned mother to send me a check; He was telling this Baptist couple to buy me a car. Don't be disappointed with God if you're not happy with the way certain things have turned out. God is aware of your situation, and He has already taken care of it. But you have to do your part to hear from Him, no matter how soft, and walk wherever He guides you. If you make a mistake or miss it, it's alright.

Just keep moving forward; God will reroute you in the same way as a GPS when you miss your turn.

Here is how God worked behind the scenes as I was obedient to do my part:

1. I had to hear God's faint voice instructing me when to speak at Chip's church.
2. I had to track down Chip's mother at another conference.
3. She had to give me her daughter-in-law's phone number.
4. I had to have the boldness to ask to speak at the church.
5. I had to show up on the Sunday right after Chip's annual youth conference.
6. I had to have the idea to sell Haiti bracelets.
7. I had to invest the money to have a booth at Lifest.
8. I needed my layover from Haiti to be in Chicago.
9. Joe's parents, who were in the Chicago area, needed to be headed to the festival.
10. I needed to meet the Baptist couple.
11. I needed my friend to be at the festival so I could ride back with him to Springfield.

As God answered my big prayer requests, I also believe God is answering your big prayer requests. Though our lives don't look the same on the outside, behind the scenes in the spiritual realm, please know that God is fighting just as hard for you. As God is fighting for you, you must also fight for yourself and walk into the fullness of His wild plans.

DON'T BE DISAPPOINTED WITH GOD IF YOU'RE NOT HAPPY WITH THE WAY CERTAIN THINGS HAVE TURNED OUT. GOD IS AWARE OF YOUR SITUATION, AND HE HAS ALREADY TAKEN CARE OF IT.

As you conclude this chapter, take a moment to reflect and show gratitude for His faithfulness. Whether big or small, dedicate some time to show your appreciation to Him. I believe the more you show your gratitude to God, the more opportunities God will give you to be grateful. God has done more for us than we can even remember.

CHAPTER 15

A BREAK TO REALITY

I quickly turned off my computer camera, muted my microphone, and broke away from my book writing cohort taking place over Zoom to answer the urgent video call on my phone. I knew it was important. It was my mother who wanted me to see my dying father as he lay there in hospice and on oxygen in Springfield, Missouri. I was just with him days earlier.

His voice was faint and slurred, but he acknowledged what I was saying. He prayed with me a prayer of rededication to Jesus for forgiveness and mercy and forgiveness towards others. I remembered the Scripture that taught us that we had to forgive those who sinned against us (Matthew 6:14), and I didn't want him to die with any bitterness. My father was a relatively new believer, coming to Christ just five years earlier. He had lived as a non-religious Jewish man almost his entire life.

"You can go back to what you're doing now," my mother said a few minutes later.

"No, I want to stay here with Dad as long as he wants. I'm in no rush. This is the most important thing for me to do right now," I responded.

She continued to hold the camera about a foot from his face as he lay there in the assisted living facility. He now weighed less than 100 lbs rather than his normal 220 lbs. I knew the end was coming, and my dream of my father traveling and speaking at churches was looking less and less likely.

With tears running down my face, in the most emotional moment I've ever experienced with him, I began to prophesy and boldly declare I would make *this* book a bestseller that would be read by millions. I knew that this message desperately needed to get out and that my father's legacy would continue through it. I declared that people in Heaven would come up and thank him for this book—people who would read it before they passed. I held onto an unfulfilled dream that my father would become a powerful evangelist for the Gospel. As I hung up, I had this strange sensation that this would be the last conversation I ever had with my father. Sadly, I was right.

I video called again the next day, but this time he was different. As I tried to speak with him, there was no response. It was as if he had mentally departed, staring wide-eyed ahead yet not flinching or responding. He didn't say a thing to me or acknowledge I was there. It was a scary blank stare that I had never seen before. Within 90 minutes, he raised his hand slightly to my mom, almost as if saying goodbye, and died moments later.

A GREATER PURPOSE

You've not yet finished this book but now know some of the hurdles, hardships, and exciting stories from my life. I received *that* call from my mother a few weeks after I started writing this book. Now that you've begun to see the journey I've gone through and some of the difficulties I've faced, maybe you can relate. I'm sure it is possible that your life may be full of challenges as well.

I now have a question for you...would you be willing to help someone you've never met and likely never will if it didn't cost you anything except for a few moments of your time?

Perhaps this person is just like you or maybe how you were a few years ago. They may be living a life not fully maximized for God. They might be a mother, a father, a brother, or a sister. They might be an entrepreneur, a student, a construction worker, an office worker, a fast-food worker, a stay-at-home parent, or even a missionary. Here is where you come in: this easy decision could result in countless people coming to know the Lord, with you getting credit for it for all eternity.

Before I tell you how you can easily help, I want to share a text message I received from an influential pastor over ten years ago in Los Angeles:

"God's hand is upon you, and He is going to use you mightily. You are part of the end-time ministry, and you are a general that He is raising up, and I know that your ministry will be powerful and touch the lives of hundreds of millions of people."

I believe this book is part of the fulfillment of that prophetic text. Before I could write any other book, whether on evangelism, generosity, business, or numerous other spiritual topics, I knew I had to share the testimonies in this book first.

I have a conviction in my heart that I am called to impact hundreds of millions of people. I invite you to be a part of this *wild expectance* I have over my life. One of the ways to fulfill my calling is by people applying the concepts shared in this book. Unfortunately, people judge a book by its cover and its reviews. Therefore, will you please take a break from reading, go to my book page on Amazon or Goodreads, and leave me an honest review of this book? Perhaps you will share what you've liked best about what you've read so far, along with a star rating? Other people will review your feedback, and what you write might make or break their decision to begin living a life of *wild expectance.*

WITH TEARS RUNNING DOWN MY FACE, IN THE MOST EMOTIONAL MOMENT I'VE EVER EXPERIENCED WITH HIM, I BEGAN TO PROPHESY AND BOLDLY DECLARE I WOULD MAKE *THIS* BOOK A BESTSELLER THAT WOULD BE READ BY MILLIONS.

I believe that if you introduce something valuable to someone, they will associate the impact that results with you. If you know someone and desire for them to experience what I shared in this book, then please bless them by sending them a copy. Don't send them the copy that you're holding because you are going to want to keep it and refer back to this book from time to time.

Know that by sharing this with others, you will begin shifting your sphere of influence into faith-filled, Spirit-led believers who will begin doing the impossible for God. I can't do this alone, but *we* can do it together. Thank you so much for reading and sharing; I look forward to the continued encouragement you will receive in the coming chapters.

CHAPTER 16

THE CHURCH ACROSS THE VALLEY

I had never seen a leg look so infected in my life. If this Haitian man did not receive a miracle, it looked as if amputation was imminent. God told him to come up to this rural area and become a pastor to these people. Now God needed to heal him so that he could fulfill his calling.

This Haitian pastor would routinely pay for a motorcycle ride from his town in order to come halfway up this rural mountain with the faith and confidence that he had heard from God. He was called to come here to start a church and open a school. He wasn't a foreign missionary, nor was he associated with a large organization that could provide outside financial aid. He was simply a Haitian man who heard from God to become a missionary to his own people.

If a poor Haitian can risk the little that he does have to reach his own people, how much more can we do to help those around us?

I had traveled to Haiti many times but had never been to this church. I had grown accustomed to taking multiple trips a year to this rural area with students from our ministry. Some of our team members had been to this church before; they were excited, explaining how this used to be a foundation with hopes of a building someday. Now we were back years later, preaching inside the church lit by a single lightbulb.

After service, the pastor showed our ministry team what appeared to be a gangrene-infected leg and asked if we could all pray for him. We gathered around him and prayed in agreement for a miracle in this man's life. We didn't have the money to send him to a hospital—there were countless practical needs of people in our own area that we couldn't meet. Nonetheless, we prayed in the name of Jesus for a healing miracle and praised and thanked God for this pastor's healing.

IF A POOR HAITIAN CAN RISK THE LITTLE THAT HE DOES HAVE TO REACH HIS OWN PEOPLE, HOW MUCH MORE CAN WE DO TO HELP THOSE AROUND US?

We didn't see an immediate change but faith-filled prayers change situations. You don't have to feel anything for your prayers to touch the heart of God and manifest healing from the spiritual into the physical. All we need to have is the confidence to pray and have the faith to let God do the rest.

THE BLIND MAN

I'm reminded of a story from a few years earlier: I was in Haiti preaching at a different church. I invited people to come forward after the service for prayer. As Haitians started coming to the front, I made my way to the left side of the line that began to form and prayed for the first man. This man was blind, and my confidence was zapped out of me as I prayed for him and saw no physical change.

Fear, anxiety, and self-judgment overtook me because I had just told the locals that God wanted to heal them, and this blind man still couldn't see! After we prayed for everyone, the blind man's friends helped to guide him out. It looked as if he was leaving just as blind as he was when he arrived. One minister later said that I should have started praying for people on the opposite side of the room first, building my faith up to the blind man as I prayed for others.

It was difficult watching this poor, elderly, blind Haitian be led out of the church. I wondered what he thought of my message. Did he think I was a fraud? How would Jesus' early disciples have responded if Jesus said people were going to get healed and nothing happened? Jesus' message wouldn't have had much credibility in the eyes of His first disciples if the blind didn't see, the lame didn't walk, and the deaf didn't hear. Ultimately, the prophecies of the Messiah in Isaiah 35:5-6 would not have been fulfilled if it weren't for His miracles. The Pharisees wouldn't have been threatened by Jesus because He wouldn't have had the masses of followers that resulted from His dynamic healing ministry. It was Jesus' miracles that helped validate His powerful message.

Why, then, was I not seeing the fruit I desired to see regarding people getting healed when I prayed for them? Have you ever prayed for someone only to have nothing happen? Have those prayer failures discouraged you from stepping out more to pray for others?

MY QUESTION ANSWERED

A month after my failed attempt to see a blind man healed through prayer, I was honored with the opportunity to have lunch with a prominent missionary, Dr. David Horton, and ask him some tough questions. David used to be Kenneth Hagin Senior's organist and was later a co-director of his healing school. Finally, he did some preaching in Kenneth's crusades before launching his own ministry. David's life was filled with incredible stories of miracles overseas, including countries like Haiti. If anyone knew the answer to my question, it would be David. I wanted to know what David's secret was when he prayed for others, which resulted in so many people experiencing divine healings or creative miracles; I wanted to know why I was not seeing the results promised to me from the Bible.

"You want my advice? You have to skip it and pray for the next one with the same boldness," he told me when I shared about the blind man.

He went on to tell me an incredible story from a preacher in Africa. Whether you believe this story or not, the principle behind it is powerful:

"There was a guy that I heard about in one of the African countries where everyone was starving to death. The 'death wagon' picked up

the dead bodies and piled them in a pile on the edge of town before they dug a hole and buried them in mass. There was this preacher who decided he wanted to raise the dead. He would go out there every morning and practice raising the dead. He laid his hands on 60 dead bodies before he got one up. He finally got it. So, he would go out there to the dead pile because he knew what time they would pile them up before they buried them. This was crazy. He would go out and drag one out and get nothing. So, he would go out the next day (and try again to raise them from the dead). He did this for a couple of months. Instead of backing up, he got bolder. I have always made myself—not that I was inspired to do it—get bolder, especially when something doesn't happen in a crusade setting."

After sharing this with me, David gave me a little book from one of his mentors, Jerry O'Dell. It was titled, *The Wonderful, Powerful Gospel of Jesus Christ: Learn How to Share or Preach the Glorious Gospel of Power!* and it outlined how to share the Gospel and pray for people in a crusade setting. If you are interested in crusade ministry, I strongly encourage you to buy this little-known gem.

David went on to say that during the crusades, they got so bold that they would declare if God did not show up and do miracles that the audience was welcome to shoo them (David and his team) out of town. I later heard another missionary tell me that he would tell his audience that if God didn't show up, the crowd could stone them. Talk about boldness!

The next day, I was introduced to another minister whom David worked with who had become a pastor. I met with this minister in his office at his church. I asked him a lot of questions about divine healing. After we met, he invited me to his service that evening.

During the service, he shared about the first time he stepped out to pray for someone. He was debating with a friend in a Chinese restaurant regarding divine healing. The question at hand was: "Do you pray for others only when the Holy Spirit tells you to, or do (you believe that) we have the freedom to pray for everyone because the Bible says to?"

"You just can't do that. That's not wisdom," his friend argued against praying for just anyone.

The pastor told his congregation that a lot of preachers who talk about wisdom regarding the supernatural power of God have a very short testimony file.

"We can't be too consumed with wisdom that we're not bold," he told the audience.

Let's return to his story:

"You *can* lay hands on the sick. You *can* preach the Gospel. You *can* get people healed," he responded to his cynical friend.

As they debated, an elderly man walked in with a crutch.

"Okay big mouth, go pray for him."

What did I get myself into? the pastor thought to himself. He was being called out on the spot.

"Come on, let's see what you got," his friend taunted as the other man finished his meal and left the restaurant. Not wanting to back down from the challenge, he ran out the door after the man.

"Sir, I'm going to pray for you. God loves you and wants to heal you! What do you think?"

"Okay, that sounds good."

"Sit down in the driver's seat. I am going to pray for your legs."

The elderly man then sat down and pulled his leg off. He was walking with a crutch because he had a prosthetic leg!

Driving home, the pastor felt really stupid. This man didn't get healed, and the pastor was embarrassed at what had happened as a result. Then, the Holy Spirit spoke clearly to him:

"See, that wasn't that bad, was it? Next time, care about *the person* and not about *your ego*."

When we pray for others, it's about showing compassion for them regardless of practical results. We can short circuit what God wants to do when we give in to the fear of what others will think of us. When we take it off of us—the pressure to see someone immediately healed—and make it about loving who we are praying for, we can then tap into the power source.

Two weeks later, the pastor saw a woman who was almost completely blind. She was using a walking stick, and his heart was completely stirred up for her.

"God loves you and wants to show that to you. This may seem a little weird, but can I pray for you?" the pastor boldly asked.

After he prayed with her, her cataracts were healed. It was a miracle. However, what if, out of insecurities and what seemed like prayer failures, he had stopped praying for others?

This pastor has had countless healing testimonies ever since this miracle. Love is what will move and activate the supernatural. Preach the Gospel message, and signs and wonders will validate it. So many times, we don't make decisions to pray for people because we are afraid of what they will think of us.

I want to reaffirm a Scripture from earlier in this book. Mark 16:20 reads, "And they went out and preached everywhere, while the Lord worked with them and confirmed the message by accompanying signs."

These two experienced ministers told me that when we preach the Gospel message, God's power is there to validate the Gospel's truth. In a world where others are experiencing the supernatural through demonic means, how much more do we need to expect the genuine?

"What if they think I am weird? What if they do not get healed? What if my friends are embarrassed by my actions?"

When you pray for someone, you are not responsible for the results (the physical manifestation of healings or other miracles). You are responsible for delivering the Gospel message and praying for people in faith and love. The bolder you are, the more you will see. The Gifts of the Spirit, as outlined in 1 Corinthians 12, are an overflow of walking in the compassion of God.

In John 5:30, Jesus himself said, "I can do nothing on My own. As I hear, I judge, and My judgment is just because I seek not My own will but the will of Him who sent me."

I want to remind you that nine chapters later in John 14:12, Jesus said, "Truly, truly, I say to you, whoever believes in Me will also do the works that I do, and greater works than these will he do because I am going to the Father."

The same power that validated Jesus's witness is available for us today. Just because someone doesn't get healed through our prayers doesn't mean that we should stop praying. When praying for others, shake off the attacks from the enemy, and resist demonic condemnation!

Just because someone doesn't immediately manifest healing, that doesn't mean God is not healing them. In Luke 17:14, Jesus heals ten lepers, but their healing does not manifest immediately: "When He saw them He said to them, "Go and show yourselves to the priests." And as they went, they were cleansed."

Again, the Scriptures tell us that as they *went*, they were healed of leprosy. If you do not see immediate healing in the people you are praying for, it is possible that they are still *wenting*; maybe that blind Haitian man was still *wenting*.

Our ministry team has prayed for countless people over the years in Haiti. The needs were so vast, and on the practical side, it looked so hopeless that you had to prevent yourself from becoming numb to the local people's suffering and difficulty. Haiti is one of the poorest countries in the world, and at the time of this experience, Haiti was the poorest country in the western hemisphere.

> SO MANY TIMES, WE DON'T MAKE DECISIONS TO PRAY FOR PEOPLE BECAUSE WE ARE AFRAID OF WHAT THEY WILL THINK OF US.

It's not uncommon to see a single mother of seven raising kids in a one-room hut by herself in Haiti. Hunger is something that Haitians have experienced their entire lives. No mother should have to choose between sending her kids to school or feeding her family.

THE HAITIAN MISSIONARY

Let's reflect back to the beginning of this chapter, where our missions team prayed for the Haitian pastor's leg. We didn't know what we would see the next time we visited this pastor's church. After all, we've had Haitian friends prematurely die from treatable causes, seen once devoted missionaries give up on their calling, and witnessed Haitians make desperate moves, like armed robbery, which they would end up regretting for the rest of their lives.

Would this pastor still be alive? Would he be on crutches and missing a leg? Would he have lost his zeal and faith in what God had called him to do on this rural mountainside? We prayed in faith with this man who desperately needed a miracle and expected that God would take care of him.

Though I've been going to Haiti for over a decade, and I've been there as many as six times in one year, there were some years that I was only able to take a few trips. This was because of civil unrest in the nation or ministry commitments back in the States. We prayed for this Haitian man during a time when our team wasn't as active in this nation. When we did make it back to Haiti, we couldn't always go back to the pastor's church because of the risk of our truck getting stuck in the mud. This concern was valid and stemmed from a story that took place before my time as a missionary. One of our mission teams had to walk back to their small dormitory (built by an American missionary) at night because their vehicle got stuck in the mud after a rainstorm. This happened after an evening service and was an incident that the team never wanted to risk again. It's dangerous walking at night in Haiti. Because of this, sporadic rainstorms made having services there challenging. Therefore, it was a year before we could come back to this church that we called the "church across the valley."

When we returned, we were relieved that the pastor was still there. During worship, we witnessed this man jumping up and down in excitement as he played his accordion.

"God healed me after your team prayed for me last year," he told us after the service through a translator.

This situation helped teach me that just because you pray for someone and you don't witness the miracle immediately, it doesn't mean that God isn't about to manifest a miracle after you've left. There might be numerous miracles that result as a byproduct of your obedience that you won't know about here on the Earth. You won't truly know your eternal impact until you arrive in Heaven, but don't allow that unknowing to stop you from stepping out and taking "risks" for God.

THE TESTIMONY IN THE DARK

Learning that God had healed this man wasn't the only thing incredible about that particular visit. I remember preaching into the darkness as the sun went down and the pastor scrambled to turn on a battery-powered light. It appeared that the locals didn't have fuel for their generator, so we couldn't use the single light bulb in the center of the room.

When I had finished preaching my message, I gave an opportunity for those who didn't know Jesus to accept Him as their Lord and Savior. As I looked into the darkness, being blinded by the light that lit up my Bible, I saw a single person raise her hand.

"I see that hand," I said, and the Haitian translator repeated.

"GOD HEALED ME AFTER YOUR TEAM PRAYED FOR ME LAST YEAR," HE TOLD US AFTER THE SERVICE THROUGH A TRANSLATOR.

It wasn't a Haitian, however, who had raised her hand for salvation. It was a Japanese international student who had been a part of our ministry's conversation circle at UCLA. She said that she wanted to come on this trip as a cultural experience and do humanitarian relief work abroad because her country didn't actively value these kinds of experiences (mission trips). This Japanese student got saved in a dark, one-room church on the mountainside in the backwoods of Haiti. What a testimony!

Once again, before we left, the pastor, whose leg was healed, shared his desire and passion for starting a school in this area. We were able to give him a small offering, but unfortunately, we did not have the resources to help this humble man of God in the way we wanted.

Whenever our ministry team would return to Haiti, I thought of this pastor and his church across the valley, even when we couldn't physically be present for service. There were various churches that needed our help, and we tried our best to accommodate as many as possible.

POLITICAL UNREST

In the years that followed, the political situation in Haiti deteriorated significantly. Not only was Haiti a nation filled with poverty, but now the little infrastructure that they did have was worsened. Also, inflation was increasing significantly, and people were rioting and demonstrating over the rising fuel prices. Gang activity and influence increased, taking over entire towns, while judges were scared to go to work, and open seats in parliament were left vacant. Elections could not be held due to the increasing violence. The US Embassy then changed the travel advisory of Haiti to Level 4, which is a do not travel advisory. This was the same designation reserved for nations like North Korea and Iran. There were constant protests demanding the resignation of President Jovenel Moïse, who was later assassinated.

With the increase in safety concerns, we decided to temporarily halt mission trips to Haiti. During this period, we pivoted our mission efforts to Vietnam, hoping that the situation in Haiti would deescalate. Then, COVID-19 devastated the world and prevented us from traveling anywhere abroad. It would be 20 months until we could return to Haiti.

CHAPTER 17

INSIDE THE 10/40 WINDOW

I hadn't been in Vietnam for a week and had already seen so much on my first mission trip to this nation. Our ministry team was at a Vietnamese pastors' conference, and the room was packed. Seating was limited, so the Vietnamese organizers had to turn away others who wanted to attend. All of these Vietnamese pastors and their staff paid to be there. The head of the Vietnamese Assemblies of God, the largest Spirit-filled denomination in the nation, was upfront and about to speak. Alongside leading the other Assemblies of God pastors in Vietnam, he had his own church he pastored.

On the Sunday before this gathering, we had been at this pastor's church (which was also where Winston had preached two powerful messages). I was blown away by what I witnessed there. This Vietnamese pastor's church met in a skyscraper, almost on the top floor. Nine people were on stage worshiping God with a talented band in both English and Vietnamese. There was a room full of Spirit-filled believers for this Sunday morning service in which everyone fervently prayed and worshiped God. They had two services, and they were both packed.

This was nothing like my experience of churches in Haiti: our team was actually inside with air conditioning, and the Vietnamese worship band sounded better than many in America! The band played fast-beat and catchy songs in Vietnamese with a talented, full worship team consisting of a lead singer, backup singers, a drummer, an electric guitar player, a bass guitar player, and people spinning flags. This church was performing some songs from Nissi United, a popular worship band in Vietnam. You can listen for yourself to some of the music played by downloading Nissi United's album "Muôn Thu Không Đổi Thay."

A few days later, our ministry team congregated at the pastors' conference. What was the head of the Vietnamese Assemblies of God going to say? I was sure that his stories were powerful. At this point, I had never heard a sermon from a Vietnamese pastor before. Judging by his age, he must have been only a kid when he lived through the travesties of what Vietnam calls the "American War."

Looking at us, he said that we were the teachers for this three-day pastors' conference. The pastors who were attending this conference were expecting four power-packed sessions a day, back-to-back. Who were *we* (myself, my brother, Winston, and a fellow missionary staff member) to be qualified to teach them? The pastor said that 70% of those in attendance had been in prison for their faith. Our ministry team lived in the United States; therefore, our life was easy compared to the pain, suffering, and persecution some of them had faced for following their faith. What the pastors did not know was that we were on a scouting trip to Vietnam (uncertain of what we would find). Our mission trip was to prepare the way for others back home to come and join us in ministry here. Looking at each other, there were just four of us in attendance.

"I guess we could all take a session each day," Winston said.

As I previously mentioned, we had been unable to go back to Haiti because of civil unrest, so we pivoted our efforts to Vietnam. Incredibly, we were able to take six trips to this communist nation in 2019. This was right before COVID-19 shut the world down and prevented us from returning. I had traveled abroad seven times that year, spending around 25% of the year inside the 10/40 window, which represents the least evangelized region in the world. Because the Lord knew about the upcoming lockdowns and travel restrictions, He enabled our team to do in 10 months what could have taken years—including speaking at over 45 church services!

Our ministry team was in the middle of Ho Chi Minh City, formerly Saigon, in South Vietnam. Winston, who was leading this trip, fled Vietnam as a refugee during the fall of Saigon. This was the first time in years since he had returned.

It was a historic moment. While we were training pastors in the south, President Trump was meeting with the President of Vietnam in the capital city of Hanoi. What made it even more historic was that President Trump was also meeting with Kim Jong Un, the leader of North Korea. Kim Jong Un traveled by train to meet Trump in Hanoi. You might have seen this on the news. I believe there was a spiritual significance that the President of the United States and the head of North Korea were both in Vietnam at the same time our ministry team was there.

UNCERTAIN WHAT LAID AHEAD

Before arriving in Vietnam, I didn't know what to expect. I had seen the Rambo movies, stories of brutality from both sides, and had heard urban legends of American prisoners of war still in camps somewhere in the vast jungles of Southeast Asia. Our ministry team was entering the only country America had lost to. I began to question if I would immediately be arrested for being American upon entering this nation. I was expecting a war-torn country antagonistic to Americans. Instead, I saw skyscrapers, Rolex shops, Gucci stores, and friendly faces everywhere we went.

When I learned that I was one of the speakers for the pastors' conference, I intently prepared for my messages and prayed that the Lord would give me the right topics to teach. I didn't have any specific messages prepared for this conference, but in actuality, I had been preparing to speak for years: documenting stories, experiences, and scriptural applications for a decade. After nearly ten years in full-time ministry, I have preached numerous times through a translator and have had the opportunity to speak across the United States and the world.

My first two teachings were on a topic I knew well—faith and miracles. As I was praying for the last day's topic, the Lord brought to my remembrance one of my online Bible school courses that I took. It taught about Paul's second missionary journey.

If you're not familiar with Paul's second missionary journey, let me share its importance. In Acts 16:6-7, Paul and his team had walked hundreds of miles without clear direction. They didn't know where they were to go, only where not to: "And they went through the region of Phrygia and Galatia, having been forbidden by the Holy Spirit to speak the Word in Asia. And when they had come up to Mysia, they attempted to go into Bithynia, but the Spirit of Jesus did not allow them."

Finally, there was a vision of a Macedonian man asking for help. At last, Paul and his team had some clear direction on their purpose. After 1,500 miles from their starting point, long days, and treacherous seas, they finally arrived. Surely, they were going to lead this man to Christ, and revival was going to break out.

Instead of finding a man, they found a small prayer meeting being led by a woman. From the looks of it, it didn't appear that there were the 10 Jews necessary to form what the Jews call a *minyan* to justify a synagogue. Initially, Paul and his team saw very little fruit, and I am sure they were discouraged.

Eventually, they were able to deliver a demon-possessed slave girl. What was the reward for delivering this girl? Unfortunately, it was embarrassment, imprisonment, and abuse. Had they missed God? At that moment, I'm sure they wanted to give up.

Similarly, these Vietnamese Christians had been through a lot, and it could have been easy (and understandable) for them to want to give up.

- Have you ever thought you missed God?
- Was there a time when you felt as if your life was unredeemable?
- Have you ever wanted to give up?

At this point in Paul's ministry, he had written only one letter. What if he had given up from discouragement? I've heard it credited that many historians attribute the spread of Christianity into Europe and the western world to Paul's answering of the ministry call into Macedonia. The enemy desperately tried to discourage Paul during this mission's journey. It is easier for the enemy to stop something at the beginning rather than when it is firmly established.

Later that year, our ministry team hosted the National American-Vietnamese Assemblies of God Conference in Southern California. We flew in the head of the Vietnamese Assemblies of God and George Wood, the head of World Assemblies of God at the time, to speak at the conference. The first three topics they taught were (similarly) faith, miracles, and Paul's second missionary journey. Before this, I had sought the Lord on what God would say to believers in Vietnam, and now the same three topics were being shared with the American-Vietnamese church! This was an affirmation that I had heard from God correctly when I diligently prayed for what I was to share during the pastors' conference on my first trip to Vietnam. I then had the

> **IT IS EASIER FOR THE ENEMY TO STOP SOMETHING AT THE BEGINNING RATHER THAN WHEN IT IS FIRMLY ESTABLISHED.**

revelation that George Wood was, in fact, the author of the Bible school book, which the Lord brought to my remembrance that inspired me to teach on Paul's second missionary journey!

A COMMITMENT TO PRAYER

The pastors' conference in Vietnam was being held at a local Assembly of God church with multiple floors. They had a music school on one level while another level was completely dedicated to prayer. I was impressed by how seriously they took prayer. They had pictures of countries around the world they were interceding for in prayer. The members of this church were even praying for the United States!

One pastor at this church would wake up every morning at 4 am and devote the entire day to prayer. Their faithfulness stirred in me a greater reality that faith-filled prayers in the name of Jesus change situations around the world, regardless of who you are or where you live. The prayer floor also had what they called "prayer tombs" (small rooms you couldn't stand in). The members there would go into these private tombs on their knees and pray.

We would later see these same private prayer rooms at another church in the Mekong Delta, located in Southwest Vietnam. The second in command of the entire Assemblies of God in Vietnam was committed to heavily investing spiritually into this poor region. He would continually make trips there from Ho Chi Minh City. The Vietnamese prayer warriors we met weren't just committed to a lifestyle of intercessory prayer for their personal lives, but they were also committed to training believers in other regions how to pray as well.

I experienced great conviction when I observed the honor some of these Vietnamese warriors held in their devotion to intercession, praying for the church, governments, and the world. They saw prayer as a necessity, not as a leisure activity. To think, the persecuted church is praying for you and me. Through persecution and difficulty, the early church grew in numbers. This great difficulty created great reliance on God, and in return, this process birthed a strong prayer life in the lives of these believers. The Vietnamese church experienced great difficulty, too, and is also growing in numbers.

I hope the testimony of these Vietnamese believers stirs in you a greater desire to pray and intercede—not just for your life, but for your family and friends' lives too. You're needed to pray for the leadership in your nation, your local leaders, and people in places of authority and influence:

THEY SAW PRAYER AS A NECESSITY, NOT AS A LEISURE ACTIVITY. TO THINK, THE PERSECUTED CHURCH IS PRAYING FOR YOU AND ME.

"First of all, then, I urge that supplications, prayers, intercessions, and thanksgivings be made for all people, for kings and all who are in high positions, that we may lead a peaceful and quiet life, godly and dignified in every way. This is good, and it is pleasing in the sight of God our Savior, who desires all people to be saved and to come to the knowledge of the truth" (1 Tim 2:1-4).

Our leaders need our prayers now more than ever. Instead of bad-mouthing those in government, we should genuinely pray for them to come to the saving knowledge of Jesus and make Godly decisions. God died for them just as He died for us, and the spiritual warfare these people face is astronomical. Their decisions impact countless people, so it's crucial we do everything we can in the Spirit to help, starting with prayer.

It was encouraging to see the younger generations especially hungry for God. During the pastors' conference, about half of the attendees were under the age of 35. One evening, we hosted a youth rally where at least 400 young people filled the church to worship God and deepen their faith. This was very encouraging and pointed to the spiritual future of this nation.

A GATHERING OF BELIEVERS

During my 5th trip back to this nation, Over 2,000 pastors and their congregants gathered for the 30th anniversary of the Assemblies of God in Vietnam. Pastors from all across Vietnam were there, coming from places we couldn't legally visit. This must have been the largest legal gathering of Assemblies of God believers ever in this nation.

During this gathering, the Communist government of Vietnam officially recognized the Assemblies of God as a legal entity in that nation. This recognition opened up the door for them to legally have church buildings, run Bible schools, and host other activities to advance the Gospel.

You would have expected this recognition to appear on the front page of every Christian news outlet. But because only a handful of Westerners and I were present, news outlets had no clue this incredible miracle had just taken place. Nearly two months had passed before anything significant was released in the media about this extraordinary development.

A MUCH NEEDED CONFIRMATION

I never imagined that I would be preaching in Vietnam and training up the next generation of spiritual leaders in that nation. But when we decide to serve God with *wild expectance*, God does things we don't always expect.

To help compensate for any insecurity I may have had as I embarked on my first journey in that nation, God did something that surprised me. I was preaching my fourth sermon in just three days. I had just finished preaching at the pastors' conference earlier that day and now was speaking to a youth group that evening. To my surprise, one of the youth in attendance was wearing a shirt that said UCLA. I had never seen a UCLA shirt in a church service outside the Los Angeles area, and this girl was wearing this shirt halfway across the world with no clue that I was a missionary on that campus. When I asked her if she knew what UCLA meant, she said she didn't and that she just liked the design. It might as well have said "Nike or "Adidas." I haven't seen another UCLA shirt worn by a Vietnamese citizen since. That shirt was something simple but very important regarding how God affirmed to me that I was on the right path. I believe God will do simple things like this in your life, too, giving you the confidence to keep moving forward in the direction He's leading you.

CHAPTER 18

THE SAND MINE MAN

During one of my trips to Haiti, before COVID-19 shut down the world, I met a Haitian man who sold his coal business to cover the medical expenses for his wife's sickness. However, even that financial sacrifice couldn't save her from a condition that was likely treatable with modern medicine. The hospital system is so bad in Haiti that people die all the time from things that are easily treatable in the United States and other developed nations. Her death left him in debt to the morgue and widowed with five girls to take care of.

In our many trips to Haiti, our ministry team had never met this man before. It seemed there were as many stars in Heaven as there were stories of loss in this nation. Yet, the believers here had a vibrant faith and love for Jesus that was stronger than many of the believers back in the United States. A young Haitian shop owner, whom we had known since he was a little kid, brought this man to us.

We had watched this shop owner grow up over the years and had helped him (financially) to get his store up and running. He was a devout believer and did everything he could to help his fellow Haitians in need. He knew that bringing this man to us might have meant there was less aid that could have gone to him, but he didn't care.

"Can you help me start my coal business again?" the widowed man asked through an interpreter. He was left without a business and a job after his wife's death. We wanted to help him and did what we could to supply his family with a suitcase of clothes. We also provided him with a large bag of rice and beans for him and his daughters.

However, we didn't have the extra money to help him get his business started again. There were others we wanted to help financially; good people we had known for years whom we weren't able to help either. We always did our best to use our limited resources wisely to help the local Haitian people. We did this through feeding programs, covering medical expenses, investing in education, helping local pastors, and countless other things. We didn't want to just give a *handout* but a hand *up;* we worked to meet immediate needs while providing long-term and sustainable solutions. We were extremely passionate about education, economic development, and job creation, but more people wanted to start businesses than we had the funding for at the time.

Back then, I remember a kid asking me for $5 to pay for his English school on the last day of a mission trip. I wanted to help him, but I had literally wiped out my bank account to come to Haiti, and I didn't have $5 left to help him. This was before I had started my business. We try to help as many people as we can until the very end, but there comes the point when we just aren't able to help anymore on each trip.

A TREACHEROUS JOB

When we returned to our rural village later that year, we went to visit the widowed man to see how he was doing. He had gotten a job working in the sand mine. Every day it was his responsibility to fill up an entire dump truck with sand in the hot, grueling sun. He said that he wouldn't get paid until this was done. With a pickaxe in hand, he and a few others would hammer the rock wall and turn it into sand. They would then fill a wheelbarrow and wheel it over to the dump truck. After five hours of piling pound after pound of sand into the truck, he would split the days' pay with his three other co-workers. The four of them collectively would get paid 1,000 Haitian Gourdes to split. Since the exchange rate at the time was $1 for every 75 Haitian Gourdes, they were paid about $13.33 to split four ways.

With his mere $3.33, he was expected to pay for food for himself and his five daughters. He couldn't afford to feed his family on this salary, much less send his daughters to school. Thankfully, we were once again able to get food and supplies into their hands. Moreover, we sponsored his daughters in the education program started by one of our UCLA alumni. Seeing his work conditions broke our hearts. We desperately wanted to help him more. "Can you help me start another coal business?" he asked again through an interpreter. We didn't have the extra resources to help. *Hopefully, on our next trip,* I thought.

AN UNPLANNED BREAK

We had plans to return to Haiti in a few months during UCLA's spring break. We didn't anticipate that civil unrest, rioting, and a global pandemic would prevent us from coming back for 20 months. I would oftentimes think about the widowed man: so many long, grueling days working in the sand mine just to survive. The Haitian shop owner had told our ministry team that the widowed man was once a successful business owner. He harvested trees and chopped them up, and turned them into coal. He filled bags, both large and small, with coal that he sold to people in the area. Coal is a daily necessity for Haitian outdoor kitchens. With a specialized skill like his, the widowed man knew that he could support his family if he was only given the resources to get started.

Many people have a specialized calling to be missionaries or to do ministry full-time. Instead of fulfilling their God-given destiny, some find themselves on the sidelines. Like the widowed man, they find themselves out of their *gifting* not because they want to be there but because nobody has given them a chance. They tried to step out into their calling, but they may have become discouraged about the mission field due to a lack of funding; these people ARE NOT BEGGARS, and they need our support. They need YOUR support.

EQUIPPING THE SAINTS

Do you know anyone from your church, work, or school who has expressed an interest in full-time ministry which you can invest in? Lives can be transformed through generosity. The widowed man faced nearly two more years of unnecessary suffering that could have been avoided if he had just had $400 to restart his business.

Despite the global pandemic and the sporadic political demonstrations in the nation, we decided to come back to Haiti because this village desperately needed help. We did this while many mission organizations you may have heard of pulled out their missionaries and humanitarian workers due to the pandemic and civil unrest. Through prayer and God's perfect timing, we decided to return.

I didn't know if the widowed man was still alive or not. The sight of the sand mine and dump truck was burned into my memory. I desired to help this man however I could but I didn't have the resources to do so on my previous trip. Our ministry team had a rhythm of going to Haiti multiple times a year, and there was a prospect of getting him the money a few months later. I just didn't know two months would turn out to be 20!

"Treat every trip like it's your last. Life is fragile," Winston would tell me when we were in Haiti.

Sometimes we get into a routine and take special moments for granted. We let the spirit of familiarity prevent us from living in the moment. We take for granted the experiences and people in our lives that are special. Are there any things in your life that you have to show more appreciation for? Take a moment to slow down, reflect, and show your gratitude to God for these things.

A MUCH NEEDED RETURN

When I finally returned for my 23rd trip to this village, a famine was in the land. The village and local people were doing worse than ever. The widowed man was continually harassed by the family of his deceased wife because his house had once belonged to her. Her family wanted his simple house for themselves and made his life miserable because of this.

Compared to the various others living in huts and tents, his two-room house was a luxury. However, the widowed man couldn't even afford locks or door handles for his home, and as a result, people would come in and continually steal the little that he did have. *Desperate people do desperate things.* His situation worsened so much that he had to send his daughters to live elsewhere because he couldn't support them and was concerned for their safety. Our friend, the shop owner, showed compassion for him and lent him $5 worth of supplies. Things were so desperate for this widowed man that he couldn't even repay him and began avoiding the shop owner. Can you imagine being so poor that you avoid someone over such a small amount of money?

THE WIDOWED MAN FACED NEARLY TWO MORE YEARS OF UNNECESSARY SUFFERING THAT COULD HAVE BEEN AVOIDED IF HE HAD JUST HAD $400 TO RESTART HIS BUSINESS.

Once again, before arriving in Haiti, I raised as much as I could and cleared out my personal bank account with the intention of investing in stories like the widowed man. Our ministry team met with him and told him we had found an investor for his business. We were able to give him the money, secure him the harvesting rights for a plot of trees, buy him the tools necessary to cut down the trees, provide large bags for him to pack the coal in, and secure his first client. What is more, we assigned him a steward to keep him accountable and to guarantee that the money he was given was used to get his business started. Additionally, we gave him the money to pay back the shop owner who had brought him to us a couple of years before.

A ROLE REVERSAL

Things were starting to finally look up for him. However, for the shop owner, business was looking grim. A few years earlier, he had a vibrant community of people who would come to his shop and pay to watch soccer and movies.

On a good night, he would make a $3 profit without working in the hot sun all day. This was in addition to his profits from his one-room shop. His business began to diminish when his television broke. He didn't have the money to repair it and lost his most profitable revenue stream. After that, he was down to $30 or less in profits each month for his entire business. Inflation rates were skyrocketing with the U.S. Dollar worth about 25% more that it was on our previous trip. Along with extreme fluctuations in the currency, there were times when the shop owner had to sell his products for less than he had paid for them. How could he run a business with such extreme fluctuations in his nation's currency?

Things were already expensive in that nation. Gas prices in Haiti are more expensive than in the United States. I've heard it said that it's more expensive to live in Haiti by American standards than back in the U.S. because everything is imported and overpriced. With poor electrical infrastructure, even the wealthy constantly need a generator and fuel. It costs our missionary team *an arm and a leg* to run the generator we purchased for the dorms we would stay at. Our local Haitian friends who owned the dorms we stayed at had many dark nights, especially during the 20-month gap until our return.

When we finally returned, our ministry team was able to hire the shop owner to be our translator for some of our services. This helped give him a little boost to get ahead, but not nearly what he needed. As much as he was struggling, various others in the village looked to him as a successful entrepreneur. He was someone they could buy their supplies from, he was one of the few local people who spoke English, and he was always pouring the little that he did have into the community around him. After returning after the global lockdowns, we did what we could on that trip to help as many as possible in that rural village.

Months passed, and our missionary team had taken multiple trips back and forth to the village that year. It was now my 4th trip since COVID-19 began and my 26th time traveling to our rural village. What I saw upon arriving in Haiti shocked me: God was blessing this shop owner in a way I had never seen from someone in his situation.

CHAPTER 19

BREAKTHROUGH IN THE JUNGLE

How was it possible that the shop owner made more money in a month and a half than he made the last year combined? His country was in the middle of a crisis, with gangs blocking supply routes, kidnapping people, and rioting over corrupt leadership. Now, only a month and a half since I saw him last, and without any outside help, he had made over $900 profit. Things like this didn't just *happen* in this village.

A month and a half earlier, I was praying about what I should teach for a church service, and I sensed that God wanted me to speak on the baptism of the Holy Spirit with the evidence of speaking in tongues. I didn't even know if they believed that at this church, but I did know that the message of Christ is universal regardless of our economic status, nationality, or background. The same is true regarding the Holy Spirit and His desire to empower us.

I put together a service on this topic, and the local shop owner was my translator.

"Do you believe speaking in tongues still happens today?" I asked my translator.

"Yes, I do," he responded.

"Have you ever prayed in tongues before?"

"No, I haven't."

"Do you want me to pray for you to receive the baptism of the Holy Spirit with the evidence of speaking in tongues?"

"Yes."

Though this is an important gift God has for all believers, He is not going to force his Holy Spirit on anyone. Some people are hesitant to receive their prayer language because of fear that God is going to force them to start speaking uncontrollably at church or work. The Holy Spirit doesn't work like that. When someone receives their prayer language, they have to actively choose to pray in tongues in the same way they have to actively choose to speak any other language. I wasn't going to pray for our translator to receive this wonderful tool unless he wanted to receive this gift. I knew I didn't have to explain the importance of praying in tongues and try to convince him this gift was for him because he had just gotten done preaching an entire sermon on it (via him translating for me). The translator desired to receive his prayer language, so I laid hands on him, prayed for him to receive it, and he immediately started praying in tongues.

"You're not praying in Creole, are you?" I asked.

"No, I'm praying in tongues," he responded.

I wanted to make sure that he wasn't just praying in his native language. I don't speak Creole very well, and though it sounded as if he was praying in tongues, I wanted to make sure.

SPIRIT-LED DEVOTION

Later during this trip, I was asked to lead devotion for our mission team. Each morning, the members of our team would gather to have a group devotion to get spiritually charged up so we could more effectively pour into the Haitians of the village. I sensed that the Lord wanted me to bring a simple message on the importance of praying in tongues every day as believers. I was speaking to experienced missionaries, some of whom had been to Haiti more times than I had. I knew all these missionaries prayed in tongues but felt impressed to speak on this topic nonetheless.

What I didn't expect was for a Haitian we had met earlier on that trip to join us for the devotion. This Haitian was friends with our primary translator and spoke great English.

"My mom prays in tongues. Can you tell me more about this?" our translator's friend asked after the devotion I led.

I began to think that maybe God wanted me to teach about speaking in tongues because He wanted me to minister to our translator's friend. Later that evening, I held an in-depth Bible study with him and went over many Scriptures on the topic. I then asked if he would like for me to pray with him to receive his prayer language. He said yes, and after we prayed, he received his supernatural prayer language just as the shop owner had.

"I can't wait to tell my mom!" our translator's friend said after he received his prayer language. This Haitian's mother was a single, white woman who had moved to Haiti by herself to run a 200+ person school. She had adopted a handful of Haitians, including him. As I taught about the Holy Spirit at different places in our rural village, it was clear that God was moving powerfully in the lives of these Haitians by pouring out His Spirit as He did in the book of Acts. However, I didn't quite understand the spiritual implications just yet.

OUR NEXT TRIP BACK

"Can you buy me a motorcycle?" a Haitian asked me through a translator on the next trip. I didn't have money to buy him a motorcycle. Besides, where was I going to find a motorcycle to buy in this village even if I had the money? He then began to talk about the shop owner, but it didn't make sense. Surely, there was a problem with translation. After all, his English wasn't very good.

Later during that trip, we visited different huts and houses, praying with people, inviting them to service, and delivering food. When we walked by the shop owner's store, I noticed a brand new motorcycle sitting out front. When we walked down the short gravel driveway to his house to visit him, I noticed someone fixing a motorcycle in his yard.

Where did this brand new motorcycle come from? I wondered. I soon learned that someone was driving through the village and had broken down right in front of his shop. When the shop owner spoke to him, he learned that the traveler was a businessman looking for a place in which he could sell motorcycles in this area of Haiti. The businessman negotiated an arrangement to give my friend, the shop owner, a commission on every motorcycle sold. My friend had already sold 9 or 10 motorcycles that month. This was incredible, but practically, how was this possible? I was excited for him but had never seen anything like that in this village. This village was located on one of two major highways in Haiti. Maybe the shop owner was able to sell these to families of important people on their way to a nearby port city. As I was reflecting on this, I had a sudden thought that I believed was from the Lord: *It's because he has been praying in tongues.*

I asked a fellow missionary on the trip about this, and he discounted the thought. Still, it stuck with me, and I really believed that God had revealed this answer to me. I decided to ask this Haitian what he thought about his newfound success.

"I think the reason God is blessing you like this is because you have been praying in tongues," I suggested.

"That is exactly right! I testified at church on Sunday about this and let everyone know the reason I have had these incredible opportunities is because I have been praying in the Holy Spirit!"

God had given him the same revelation and had confirmed what I was already sensing.

When we pray in tongues, we can pray out God's perfect will for our lives. This Haitian was generous; he loved to worship God and was a prayer warrior. I'm sure he prayed over his life and business all the time. I imagined him praying to sell more hot sauce, sodas, and rice. However, maybe God wanted him to sell motorcycles, own a repair business, and make more money working for himself than he ever had in his life. In James 4:2-3, it says that we *have* not because we *ask* not. When the shop owner prayed in tongues, God was able to bring forth this exciting opportunity and the people willing to buy from him. This Haitian's testimony is yet another example of how God's ways are bigger than our ways. The shop owner probably never fathomed selling motorcycles but when he started praying in tongues, God brought the right opportunity to him. God doesn't just have bigger plans for this shop owner in Haiti, but He has bigger plans for you as well, regardless of your nationality or social status. We need to be open to expanding our vision for our lives, and to the new opportunities He brings to us.

A GOD DIRECTED SERMON

My heart was still burdened for the church across the valley. However, yet again, it didn't look like we were going to be able to have a service there. Rain clouds could be seen forming above the mountain, and our team did not want to risk a repeat of years earlier when the truck got stuck in the mud, and everyone had to walk back. It was even more dangerous now, with risks of rioting and kidnapping that resulted from the civil unrest in the nation. To make things even worse, the Haitian *Ra-Ra* celebration had just started.

Ra-Ra is a demonic celebration in Haiti in which mobs of people walk from town to town, making large amounts of noise at night, playing instruments, dancing, drinking, and practicing Voodoo rituals. Voodoo priests from different communities are said to invoke demonic spirits to protect the bands in the evenings as they travel from town to town. The *Ra-Ra* celebration takes place the week before Easter.

I asked our translator what they were celebrating. He responded, "They are celebrating that Jesus did not resurrect from the dead, and it celebrates those who mocked Christ before His death."

I didn't want to get stuck in the middle of a *Ra-Ra* march at night as a "rich" American, especially returning from service at a time when kidnappings and desperation seemed to have risen to an all-time high.

Sometimes, bad things happen to good people, not because of God's will, but because they made bad decisions. I believe that God can guide us out of dangerous situations, but we have to be obedient to His guidance. Nevertheless, I had a strong urge from God to visit the church across the valley and tried multiple times over multiple trips, but nothing panned out. I knew we had to go.

I felt called to head to this church to deliver an offering to this pastor on behalf of our team. I remembered how the pastor had asked us for money to send kids from the area to school on our last visit, but we couldn't afford to do this. After seeing the continual deterioration of Haiti over the past five years, I couldn't even imagine the dire situation this pastor must have been left with.

Was there still a church there? Was this pastor even alive? Those are the kinds of questions our ministry team, unfortunately, had to ask ourselves year after year. I believed in my heart that he was okay and even brought an offering that I hoped to give to him. I sensed the Lord had given me a specific number. I didn't tell anyone else because I feared that they would attempt to dissuade such generosity toward a single person.

SOMETIMES, BAD THINGS HAPPEN TO GOOD PEOPLE, NOT BECAUSE OF GOD'S WILL, BUT BECAUSE THEY MADE BAD DECISIONS. I BELIEVE THAT GOD CAN GUIDE US OUT OF DANGEROUS SITUATIONS, BUT WE HAVE TO BE OBEDIENT TO HIS GUIDANCE.

While preparing for my message, I experienced excitement stirring in my heart from the transformation I had just seen in the shop owner's business. I knew I had to let others know. Just think of the transformation this could have for the people on that mountain if they received the Holy Spirit. I began to ponder whether there was a better way to articulate this powerful truth than how I was already explaining it.

I immediately thought of the famous German evangelist Reinhard Bonnke. He had extensive experience preaching the Gospel and on the Holy Spirit across Africa. His ministry *Christ for All Nations* (or CfaN for short) said Reinhard's last crusade attracted 1.7 million people over a five-day event.

Although phone service and internet in the village we were staying at were very spotty, I brought an internet hotspot with me, and at times, I was able to connect to some slow internet.

Maybe I can find a video of Reinhard preaching about the Holy Spirit and the topic of speaking in tongues in a crusade setting, I thought.

This rabbit trail eventually led me to a podcast from his successor, Daniel Kolenda. His podcast discussed the last thing Reinhard had shared with him before he had passed.

While listening to the podcast, I thought to call my friend Daniel King. I was in the middle of the jungle, but his name came to mind. I didn't know if he was available because he was constantly doing his own ministry crusades around the world. He had personally led over 1 million people to Christ through mass evangelism. It wasn't uncommon for him to attract crowds of 50,000 people or more to his services. He even attended one of Reinhard's crusades in Africa before he passed away and was at his public funeral.

At the end of the podcast, Daniel Kolenda said that if you were being called to be an evangelist, you should attend his evangelism boot camp in Orlando. I had never heard of his school until this moment, but it seemed like a great opportunity to get practical experience in the area of mass evangelism overseas.

I stepped away from listening to the podcast and called Daniel King. He didn't answer, so I decided to text.

Me: "Just tried calling you from Haiti."

Within the hour, he responded by text.

Daniel: "I'm teaching evangelists this week in Orlando. How is Haiti going?"

Me: "We fed 230 people yesterday and had two services. We have two more services today, and I'm going up to this church up in the mountains to teach on the Holy Spirit."

Daniel: "Awesome. I'm praying for an outpouring of the Holy Spirit."

Me: "You got a second?"

Daniel: "No, I'm about to start teaching."

Me: "Oh, you're actually in the middle of it, lol. You teaching the CFAN boot camp?"

Daniel: "Yeah. I'm teaching several sessions each day. 100 evangelists."

While praying in the Spirit, the Lord led me to a podcast I'd never heard before. This podcast happened to talk about an evangelism boot camp. In the middle of the podcast, I thought that I should reach out to a friend of mine. My friend Daniel was one of the keynote speakers for that same evangelism school which I had just heard about minutes earlier. Talk about reaching out to the right person at the right time!

As I've said before, remember that the voice of God can come as a sudden awareness followed by a unique conviction. I could have easily missed what God was trying to do.

My friend Daniel had just gotten back from a crusade himself overseas and agreed to talk to me between training sessions. Even though Daniel was in the middle of teaching at a multi-day conference, he took my call from the jungle to talk about evangelism. I asked him about his methodology for preaching about the Holy Spirit in an overseas setting. I explained that I was about to go to the church across the valley and asked him about his experiences preaching on the Holy Spirit overseas.

"I like to teach about God's three greatest miracles in the Bible: Creation, Calvary, and Pentecost," he shared with me.

"At creation, God created you; at Calvary, God saves you; at Pentecost, God empowers you. Creation is where we see God the Father do His greatest work. Calvary is where we see God the Son do His greatest work, and Pentecost is where we see God the Holy Spirit do His greatest work. We need all three in our lives today. A lot of Christians know God created them and know God saved them, but now, let's talk about the third dimension where God gives you His power to do what you're called to do."

This was so simple! I had the sermon I was going to preach that evening, but this sermon was better. The simplicity of this message about God's three greatest miracles shouldn't only be shared overseas in rural villages but in our workplaces, schools, and evangelistic meetings across the entire world.

Our missions team had a few different translators we rotated through for our services. The shop owner happened to be the Haitian who was translating for us that night. While we were driving up the mountain, I had another idea: ask my translator to testify at the end of the sermon about how he had recently received the baptism of the Holy Spirit and the impact this experience had made on his life.

When we finally arrived at the church, we were shocked by what we saw. I expected to see huts surrounding a small church on a small dirt lot.

"Have any Americans come here to help since we've been gone?" I asked the pastor.

"No, your group is the only foreigners who have ever visited my church," he responded.

Since I wasn't sure if this was true, I asked the translator privately. He affirmed that no other foreigners had ever been to his church.

The last time we had been there, only a one-room church building stood on the small lot. Now, the site was unrecognizable. Beautiful buildings stood everywhere, painted with vibrant blue colors. There were also attractive homes scattered along the side of the road as we approached the church. They had giant school buildings with plenty of classrooms, an administration building, multiple restrooms with running water, and what appeared to be an outdoor cafeteria. This school facility was better than the one built by the Haitian pastor on the property where we stayed when we would come to Haiti. How was this possible?

He explained that he kept praying for the people of that area and would write letters to various organizations. Finally, he persuaded an organization to help him. It was actually through the help of one of his church members who was somehow connected to a charitable organization. Sometimes it's through those you are called to help that unlocks the answers to your deepest prayer requests. This organization sent Haitian engineers to survey the ground and build the houses. He said that at every place they built houses, they would also build a school. The pastor asked if the organization wanted to come and visit, but they responded to just send back some rocks from the property.

As I walked inside the one-room church, I saw a banner hanging up at the front behind the pulpit that read "Compassion." The pastor explained how some of the school's enrollees were able to get godparents in America to send them to school. The school had somehow got Compassion International to sponsor some of the children.

I immediately knew the significance of this because Compassion International was a major sponsor of the Christian rock festivals I used to tour. The organization was constantly raising money from the stage for kids like these across the world. There are always more kids on the waiting list than sponsors available, and even getting on the waiting list was difficult. Yet, in the middle of nowhere in Haiti on this mountainside, the faith of this pastor (who was a missionary to his own people) made way for some of these children to go to school.

A friend of mine was actively speaking on behalf of Compassion International and raising money to send kids to school. As I looked in awe at the banner, I texted my friend from the mountainside and thought about how he might be raising money for some of the children at this school!

SOMETIMES IT'S THROUGH THOSE YOU ARE CALLED TO HELP THAT UNLOCKS THE ANSWERS TO YOUR DEEPEST PRAYER REQUESTS.

This pastor had heard from God to become a missionary to his own people and to ride a motorcycle up the mountain to reach this secluded area. God had placed in his heart to start a school in this poor mountain region. The only Americans who had ever been there were on our team, and we hadn't been able to come since before COVID-19. The times we did come, we were able to help a little, but nothing significant.

Now, this Haitian pastor had a church and school complex nicer than the one where our missionary dorms were located and nicer than many of the other schools we'd seen locally. If God could intervene on behalf of this man's unrelenting faith and obedience towards this poor mountain village in the middle of nowhere Haiti, what couldn't He do? Whatever situation you're facing is nothing compared to what this man had to go through, and God provided for him still.

This pastor's mindset and audacity were different from many of the other Haitians we've met. He had a vibrant bulldog faith mixed with tenacity, action, and expectation that God would see him through. His *wild expectance* wouldn't allow him to give up even when our ministry team was unable to provide the provision he needed to start a school. Instead, he looked to God as his source.

When I finished preaching, I invited the shop owner to come up and testify as planned. We then invited everyone who wanted to receive the baptism of the Holy Spirit with the evidence of praying in tongues to come forward for prayer. After our team laid hands on everyone and prayed for them, I gave the pastor the offering the Lord had placed on my heart earlier that week.

I would have liked to stay longer, but by this point, it was pitch black in the church other than the small battery-powered light on the pulpit. We needed to get out of that area for safety reasons and get back to where we were staying. As our team loaded into the back of our van, I knew that God had just moved in a powerful way amongst these people, and I believed that many who came forward for prayer were filled with the Holy Spirit. In the same way that we didn't see the healing of the pastor until a year later, I believe there were things set in motion in the spiritual realm that I might not know for years.

CHAPTER 20

THE WILD RIDE DOWN

I was in a public speaking class my freshman year of college and still remember a conversation. I was talking with another business major, and what he said shocked me: "I wouldn't mind throwing a couple of grannies on the street if it made me a million dollars," my classmate said. Who does he think he is to have such an awful mindset!? It sounded like this cocky student only cared about making money and that he would do anything to get rich, even if it meant kicking someone's grandparents out of their house. Growing up, my family had been kicked out of multiple homes, so his comment especially triggered me. This negative view of this college student was ingrained into my mind for the next four years.

In my senior year, I decided to visit another student ministry on my campus. There *he* was on stage talking about Jesus. I knew who *he* was. He said he was a Christian now, but deep down, I knew *he* wanted to throw some grannies out of their house!

Have you ever said something stupid you wish you hadn't? Chances are we've all done or said stupid stuff we regretted or didn't remember. What's worse is that the people who saw us do something or say something regrettable probably think that is who we are today.

Just think of people from your childhood—maybe a bully or a jerk from high school. When you think about that person, you might imagine them as that person from "way back when." But that's not who they are, and that's not who you are in the present day. We've all changed, hopefully, for the better.

If you have thoughts of resentment, bitterness, or unforgiveness against people from the past, you need to let them go. If you have resentment, bitterness, or unforgiveness against yourself for something you've done and regretted, repent to God if you haven't yet and forgive yourself. Jesus died on the cross to wipe away the sin of whatever you have done. You can't beat yourself up anymore. Doing so plays into the hands of the enemy and negates the power of Jesus' sacrifice in your life.

A CHANGED MAN

I would sometimes think about my former classmate. After being bombarded by Christian post after Christian post on my social media newsfeed, I finally accepted that he probably did change and have a legitimate encounter with God. I always remembered him as the tall, frat, playboy, salesman. However, God had truly changed him, and I had to let go of my past impression of him. I had met a lot of people in my college career, but that memory of him stayed with me.

I was going to be back in Springfield and thought about reaching out to him. I was back in Missouri fundraising, so I texted him and asked if we could connect. I told him I wanted to share the vision God had put on my heart for ministry. He said that he wasn't taking on any new missionaries at the time, but I said that was alright. I still wanted to connect with him, so he agreed.

I wanted to deepen my friendship with him, not because I wanted to get something from him, but because I wanted to invest in him. We met for dinner at a local restaurant, and I asked him if he was familiar with praying in tongues. He told me he had just received this gift soon after coming home from a mission trip to Africa. We then entered into a deep spiritual conversation.

"You're the only one I could have had that conversation with," he told me afterward.

He had been a part of a great campus ministry, but they didn't teach on the Holy Spirit. As a result, he had just had this incredible experience but didn't know where to go. Then, God placed me in his path.

He was no longer the "granny thrower" in my mind. He was an entrepreneur, passionately pursuing God in his life with a desire to impact his sphere of influence for the Gospel. God had transformed him into someone unrecognizable from my freshman year in college. His name was Landon, and we became close friends.

I had just finished reading the book, *The Walk of the Spirit - The Walk of Power: The Vital Role of Praying in Tongues* and had been telling everyone about it. I had an extra copy in my car, which I gave to him. The Lord told the author of the book I gave to Landon that the information in the book was so valuable that the author could no longer sell it. Because of this, the book is available online for free, which you can find with a quick Google search of the title. I recommend you read it.

IF YOU HAVE THOUGHTS OF RESENTMENT, BITTERNESS, OR UNFORGIVENESS AGAINST PEOPLE FROM THE PAST, YOU NEED TO LET THEM GO.

One time Landon had me stop by his business and pray for a salesperson of his who wanted to receive the baptism of the Holy Spirit. At that moment, Landon's office became a prayer meeting, and we prayed for his salesperson to receive his prayer language. The salesperson started praying in tongues in the middle of work hours in his boss's office!

When leaders in business, politics, and media have a powerful encounter with the true living God, there will be a ripple effect that will transform companies, nations, and Hollywood from the top down.

AN UNEXPECTED CONNECTION

Later, after Landon and I had become friends, I received a phone call from my friend Joe. "We are coming to Springfield with a Stork bus. Do you know of a place I can stay?" he asked.

I would normally have Joe and his team stay at my friend's parents' place, but for whatever reason, something just didn't seem right about that suggestion. I would stay with Landon whenever I would come back to Springfield and thought I should ask Landon if Joe and his team could stay at his place. Landon had a large house to accommodate visitors and said he and his wife wanted it to be a home that welcomed people from the ministry.

This seemingly simple act of obedience to the Lord led to a series of unexpected events. The introduction I made eventually led Joe to invest in one of Landon's businesses. This investment prevented Landon's business from going bankrupt and provided enough financial infrastructure to pivot his door-hanger marketing company into the digital marketing world.

Not too long later, I received a devastating blow from my largest donor in the form of an unexpected email. The email from my largest donor said he was consolidating his giving to a single organization. Because of this, I would only receive support for another couple of months. This was a difficult email to receive. I couldn't afford to lose their support! Not only was this going to hurt me, but it was going to hurt the donations I was making with that money. I was giving half of it away to help other missionaries as well. Now everyone who benefited from this organization's generosity was going to be hurt by the decision.

After I received the rejection letter from my largest donor, Landon told me that one of his salespeople had just sold my largest donor's business online advertising for the same amount of money that I was going to be losing monthly! When I heard that, I knew I had to change my fundraising strategy.

As I reflect on this story, I'm reminded of 1 Kings 17:2-9, when God declared a drought over Israel, told Elijah to drink from the brook Cherith, and that ravens were to bring him food. Eventually, the drought got so bad that the brook Elijah was drinking from dried up, and the Ravens stopped bringing him food. Then, the LORD gave Elijah a new command, which was crazy to any logical thinker. God told Elijah to go to Zarephath to be taken care of by a starving widow. Zarephath was located about 100 miles from the brook Cherith and just eight miles south of Sidon, which was the birthplace of Queen Jezebel, who was trying to kill Elijah.

What's the lesson here? Do not box in how God wants to provide for you. Just because God has done things a certain way in the past does not mean that is how God wants to do things in the future. Don't compare yourself to others or your past. Everyone is on their own unique journey that is constantly changing.

Thankfully, the Lord was already on top of the situation and had provided for me in an unexpected manner. God had told Landon to donate to me a marketing dealership worth $10,000. This gave me the right to sell his advertising services in the Los Angeles area. People had already paid $10,000 in other markets, and I was getting this for free. This is how I began my journey selling online advertising to local businesses alongside doing my full-time mission efforts.

> **DO NOT BOX IN HOW GOD WANTS TO PROVIDE FOR YOU. JUST BECAUSE GOD HAS DONE THINGS A CERTAIN WAY IN THE PAST DOES NOT MEAN THAT IS HOW GOD WANTS TO DO THINGS IN THE FUTURE.**

As I started selling advertising to local businesses to help finance my missions, I found that it was easier to sell a business online advertising every month than it was to get someone to support my mission work monthly for a fraction of the amount.

I had been far removed from the business world since graduating college, and this was *exactly* what I needed. I would sell advertising to a local business, and Landon's team would then actively manage the ad campaigns. I would manage the relationship with each business I sold advertising to and coordinate any ongoing campaign changes back to Landon's team. I joined the Beverly Hills and Santa Monica Chamber of Commerce and proceeded to connect with business owners along with carrying out my missionary efforts. One client even donated some new tires for my vehicle because he believed in the mission work I was doing.

It seemed as if this was working, but after a few years of this, I felt as if I was stuck in a rut. For example, I wasn't making enough money for it to be sustainable. Furthermore, the margins weren't high enough, and my sales process led me to believe that I should try to work with every business instead of focusing on a specific industry. I found it difficult competing against other marketing agencies that specialized in specific niches. For example, I once lost a large bid with a rehab facility to a competing marketing agency that had multiple rehab facilities under management and case studies that went with it. I instead had a variety of scattered case studies that may or may not be relevant.

RECRUITING FOR SAVE THE STORKS

During this time, Joe yet again tried to hire me. Ever since we had started Save the Storks (Storks), he had been trying to get me to move to Colorado to work with him full time. Meanwhile, his job offers were getting more and more tempting: "I will give you an office, a salary, and build a team around you. You'll only have to do what you're good at," Joe explained.

Get behind me, Satan! It was a great cause but not my full-time calling. I was passionate about Storks, but in this season, God was calling me to reach students at UCLA and soon USC. Joe eventually asked if I could just recruit speakers for the organization. Storks was growing rapidly and had recently brought on some high-profile speakers. Instead of being paid a salary, I would be paid for the success of the team I had recruited. I agreed to this because I really believed in this ministry and still wanted to help. I knew the Storks origins story by heart because I had lived it.

After touring Christian rock festivals one summer, Joe, myself, and a handful of others went on a mission trip to New York City to work with a local crisis pregnancy center located in the Bronx. This crisis pregnancy center had a van with a mobile sonogram inside and would park it outside of a local abortion clinic. The van provided women with scheduled abortions an opportunity to see their baby before they went into the abortion clinic. The van seemed decrepit, yet, it was making a significant impact in the lives of women in the area. Joe and I were surprised that these women would board this van with strangers. Regardless, the women who WERE getting on board would see a picture of their baby, and as a result, over half of the women would choose to keep their baby.

Joe's vision was to take this idea to cities around the nation, but instead of using decrepit vans, the ministry would sponsor beautiful Mercedes-Benz Sprinter vans with leather seats and state-of-the-art sonography equipment. The next summer, our tour involved raising money for our first "Stork Bus," but we had no clue if anyone would care and if we could actually raise funds necessary to make this dream a reality.

By the time Joe had asked me to recruit speakers for the organization, it was a well-oiled machine with Stork buses around the nation. Storks was able to calculate that for a small monthly donation, a mother and her baby could be saved from abortion. Unfortunately, the speakers I was recruiting were not having the kinds of success necessary for this to be sustainable. What is more, they had difficulty booking services, and when they did speak on behalf of the organization, they had difficulties getting people to become monthly partners.

Because I couldn't commit fully to Storks, I had to delegate speaking and training opportunities to my team. There were speaking engagements I couldn't attend and training conferences I couldn't be a part of. This was difficult, especially the time when I had to turn down a training opportunity facilitated by Storks from one of the world's top public speaking experts. I had to turn things like this down because I had conflicting commitments with my local ministry and trips abroad to Haiti. Because of this, I focused mainly on recruiting speakers and having them take speaking opportunities that would arise. This was hard because I was good at sharing the story and knew that if I took the engagements, they would go well.

I had to get creative, and finally, it looked as though I had some break-throughs. For instance, I recruited one person who seemed to have the ability to book a lot of large services and booths at Christian events. I had another friend who was already doing something similar for his local crisis pregnancy center. However, the only way to get him to speak for Storks full-time was for my speaker recruitment business to offer him a job.

Although Storks did not have speakers working directly for them, I believed in my friend and took a risk. I offered him a job with a sign-on bonus. I didn't have the money for the bonus, so I took it out of a line of credit from my marketing business.

He was soon able to start booking church services and attend training on my behalf. He was able to get a prominent advertising company to donate digital billboards across Missouri, he got Storks featured on the front cover of a Christian magazine, was able to obtain promotional radio spots around the country, and many other things to advance the cause. My friend got Stork packets into the hands of prominent musicians, speakers, influencers, and even Hollywood actor and activist Kirk Cameron.

With all the work he was putting in, I was sure this would save many babies and that my financial risks would eventually pay off. This would result in making a livable wage that would help finance my missionary efforts. However, it was very unwise to go into more debt each month by continuing to float his salary to promote this organization that I loved.

THE WOMAN AT THE BEACH

Finally, it looked as if I was about to have a breakthrough. I could hear the waves of the ocean as I sat across from the blind woman in Malibu. We were eating at a nice restaurant on the beach. She loved the sound of the ocean and liked to eat there whenever she was in town. I was encouraging her to become a Stork's speaker.

That Sunday, she was speaking at four services for a megachurch in California. She had an international following, spoke at churches around the nation, and did corporate training with prominent organizations like Dave Ramsey's. She had done an average of 75 corporate training sessions a year for over a decade. Zig Ziglar, one of America's most influential motivational speakers, even wrote a forward for her first book. Her story was so powerful that the first time she spoke for Zig, he was seen weeping afterward. This was only the second time his team had seen Zig cry (the first was at the news of the death of his dear friend Mary Kay Ash, the founder of the famous direct sales cosmetics line).

I was meeting with Gail McWilliams and her daughter. When Gail told me her story, I was astonished. I now understood why she was so popular.

"When I was pregnant with my second child, my doctor told me there was a health complication. My doctor said I had two choices, either abort my child or go blind. I said that I would never have an abortion," Gail explained.

"What a foolish decision," the doctor said as she slammed the file closed and rushed out of the room in disgust.

"Really, what she was asking me, Bryan, was to choose between legacy and convenience."

Wow. This woman considered the ability to see as a convenience over the idea of having an abortion.

"I made the decision to have my baby and ended up having five children. I eventually went completely blind. My second daughter, the one they wanted me to abort, was the first one to get married, and now she has three children," Gail went on to tell me.

When Gail decided to keep her child, she wasn't just saving her baby. She was saving an entire lineage! That daughter she saved now has a fourth child.

The enemy has worked very hard over the years to destroy lineages. Look at the story of the Israelites in Egypt: what if Moses' mother had listened to the pharaoh and killed her baby? Who would God have raised up to free the Israelites from bondage? Who would have written the first five books of the Bible? Who would God have given the Ten Commandments to? These are all scenarios that would have happened differently if Moses' mother had not let her son live.

Gail eventually became one of our speakers and spoke at a prominent pro-life conference later that year on behalf of Storks.

THE LONG ROAD DOWN

One day while driving to UCLA, I received a call from the first speaker I had ever recruited. We were working closely together to help him get speaking engagements:

"They can't find the check," he told me.

He had paid money to have a booth at a large Christian event, but the organizers had lost his payment.

"If they don't receive their payment immediately, it will cause problems for Storks," he explained. "Once they find the original payment, you will get reimbursed immediately."

I didn't have any reason not to believe my speaker. He was introduced to me through a respected acquaintance I knew from my time on the road touring Christian rock festivals. I was young and naive at the time, and I later learned that he was scamming me. He had got both me and Storks to send him money at various times. He was the master at deceiving people, and this appeared to be a chronic habit. I'm not going to go into the details, but he ended up costing Storks and myself a lot of money. When Storks realized it would cost the organization more in attorney bills to prosecute him than the money he had stolen, not to mention the time involved, they decided to drop the case and move on. At that moment, I knew I wasn't going to get my money back either.

REALLY, WHAT SHE WAS ASKING ME, BRYAN, WAS TO CHOOSE BETWEEN LEGACY AND CONVENIENCE.

A short time later, a crucial team member at the Storks headquarters decided to quit. He directly oversaw the ambassador program that worked with me and my speakers. The reason he quit was that he wanted to return to his previous profession, working for the government.

I later learned he wasn't properly reimbursing me. It wasn't malicious but an administrative shortcoming that resulted from him taking a job way over his head. By the time we realized this, he was long gone from the organization. Therefore, it was impossible to determine what I was actually owed.

His absence left a void in the speaker recruitment program. I didn't want to move to Colorado and take over the role, and Joe was too busy managing numerous other things at the time to help. I realized that I would have to lay my friend off. I had originally recruited him from his local crisis pregnancy center, but he wasn't able to raise the money necessary for me to keep paying him.

At least I still had Gail, I thought to myself.

Gail had a powerful story, and I knew that working with her would help launch my travel ministry when God released me to do so. She was inspiring me to be a better person and was living the life of a full-time speaker: she was constantly traveling and speaking at large churches and corporations across the United States while making a significant impact on those who attended her events. I knew having her voice in my life would make me a better leader, challenge me to draw closer to God, and that my friendship with her would open up bigger opportunities for ministry in the future.

In addition, her success with Storks would more than compensate for everything else that was falling apart! Storks continued to contract her to do some big events which would eventually cover the debt I had incurred.

Then the unthinkable happened. Right before my December mission trip to Haiti, I received a call from her daughter. "Gail has been diagnosed with breast cancer, and it doesn't look good," she explained. I later learned that her heart was operating at only 11%, and because of this, she had refused treatment. Before the end of the month, she was gone.

All this calamity happened very fast. What was I going to do? Though I still had my health, I felt like Job from the Bible after he lost his children and possessions. Worse still, I was nearly $50,000 in debt. I had tried my best and had failed. How could I have known that the first person I recruited was going to steal from me? How could I have predicted that my friend, who was already a pro-life speaker, was going to fail? After all, before I hired him, he had phenomenal success raising money for his local pregnancy center.

Then, when I finally received my big break by connecting with the most amazing woman I had ever met, she abruptly died about a month after her diagnosis. I once again was at my lowest moment, having been devastated through this whole ordeal emotionally, spiritually, and financially. I didn't share with those closest to me the true nature of my financial situation.

How could a good God allow all this disaster to happen, you may be asking? The answer is because we live in a fallen world. None of this was God's fault. God is the answer, not the problem. When you're at rock bottom, you should press into God, not back away.

I was on a Haiti mission trip in mid-December, right before Gail died. I knew it didn't look good for her. I went to the roof of the dormitory we were staying at to pray for her and think. Later that week, I was walking on the streets of Haiti, looking at the poverty and reflecting on how I could make an impact there. Most importantly, I was trying my best to raise money to help these people, but I wasn't able to make the impact that I desired. Even though we had Haitian friends die from treatable causes and people in this nation were starving to death, the world didn't seem to care. Millions had flooded into Haiti, but not to this village.

"Why don't you start your own marketing company?" Winston asked as we walked.

Though I hadn't shared with anyone what I was going through, and he had no clue of my situation, he saw that I was struggling financially. Winston's advice affirmed what I already thought God was leading me into. Winston was the same person my brother told me to call when I believed God was leading me into full-time ministry. This time, I was launching into Spirit-led entrepreneurship to help complement my mission work and get me out of my financial situation.

CHAPTER 21

SUCCESS
AT LAST

I flew back to America and was in St. Louis for Christmas with a plan of action. I asked my uncle if he would allow me to run advertising for his practice. He graciously agreed. The only problem was that I didn't know how to run an advertising company by myself. I had always sold advertising in the past but was never the person doing the technical work on the backend. Although I invested some money over the past few years in general online marketing strategy, I had never invested in a course that detailed the technical specifics of actually launching online ads.

A month earlier, as I watched my speaker recruitment business begin to take a nosedive, I noticed a post in a Facebook group that I believed might be my way out. I had been actively involved in different online Facebook groups and saw someone talk about the success they had running ads for chiropractors. I learned that this individual had a course on the subject, and I decided to purchase it when I returned from Haiti. He had a proven system that worked, and the course involved group coaching for me to get help when I was stuck.

The course was a lot more difficult than I was expecting. I was trying my best to do exactly what the course said, but I wasn't having the success other people were having. It was frustrating, and it felt like I was doing something wrong. Then I received a text message alerting me that someone had filled out the online form I was advertising. It worked!

I was able to get a complete stranger to schedule an appointment with my uncle and come in for a consultation. As the new patients started pouring into my uncle's practice, he referred me to another chiropractor in a nearby city who used to work for him. I used that opportunity to slightly increase my prices. I had success in getting this second chiropractor new patients too! From there, he referred me to another chiropractor in a different state, and he referred me to another in a different state, and it all snowballed from there.

I learned that the reason I wasn't having the success I desired in the beginning wasn't that I was doing something wrong; instead, it was because the area I was advertising in was a very saturated market. I was literally advertising down the street from a chiropractic college. New students were constantly graduating and deciding to open up their practice in the same city as my uncle. Other cities that I began to advertise in exploded with so much success that the chiropractor couldn't handle all the leads that were coming in. At one point, I learned that some practices were firing me not because I wasn't doing a good job but because they were overwhelmed with new patients. One doctor said he had two consecutive weeks of record-high new patients after we turned on the ads.

From there, I started running Facebook and Instagram ads for myself to get chiropractors to reach out to me. This was much easier than having to get up early to attend Chamber of Commerce meetings, networking late in the evening, and trying to get random people to buy my marketing plans. I now understood why successful entrepreneurs didn't need business cards. I had more business than I could handle.

I learned that the online marketing environment was constantly changing with updates to social media platforms, new technology, and even new ad platforms. Because of this, I continued to invest in new programs from various online marketers over the years in order to stay up to date on the latest methods and remain competitive in the market. Since then, I have invested more in online marketing strategies than in my entire 4-year college degree in entrepreneurship. This process taught me that if you want to get good at something, find someone you can learn from and pay them for their knowledge. Ultimately, I learned more about entrepreneurship by reading books from successful entrepreneurs and buying online courses than from my college degree.

THE SECRET SUCCESS FORMULA

Proverbs 4:7 teaches, "The beginning of wisdom is this: get wisdom, and whatever you get, get insight." I want to share some of the wisdom I've learned on my journey into entrepreneurship. Most businesses struggle to get new clients because they don't have the wisdom on how to grow their business on demand. However, once the concept of online marketing is understood, the hardest part of many businesses becomes easy. An important principle I learned is that a business, ministry, or non-profit should never have a *growth* problem; they should never have problems finding new clients, church members, or even prospective donors. If there are problems, they should always be operational. The majority of their issues should be about fulfilling services sold, nurturing the relationship of the new church attendees, or cultivating prospective volunteers and donors.

I LEARNED MORE ABOUT ENTREPRENEURSHIP BY READING BOOKS FROM SUCCESSFUL ENTREPRENEURS AND BUYING ONLINE COURSES THAN FROM MY COLLEGE DEGREE.

For example, if you want to make $1,000,000 this year, all you have to do is reverse engineer what that looks like. If you're a high-end coach selling group coaching for $5,000, then you only need 200 new customers a year (which averages to about four individuals a week). When you break these numbers down, your goal becomes more manageable.

But how do you get four new coaching clients a week? If you're able to convince one out of five meeting attendees to join your program, then you need 25 sales meetings a week, or five meetings per day, and then you can take the weekends off. If 50% of the people you schedule a meeting with show up, then you need to schedule 50 meetings a week. But how do you schedule

50 meetings a week, you might ask? That sounds like a lot of people! Advertising platforms are constantly changing, but the strategy remains the same: you determine where your ideal customer spends their time online and then advertise on that platform, offering something to your ideal customer in exchange for their contact information.

To do this effectively, you need to determine what your cost per lead is when advertising on these platforms. Based on the numbers I presented above, if you can get a lead for $15, then $30 will get you an appointment scheduled on your calendar and $60 will get you one appointment that actually happens, and $300 will get you that $5,000 sale. If you need 200 clients to reach your million-dollar goal, you just need to spend $60,000 on online advertising.

Once you develop an effective marketing system, you can get creative—you can hire people to make the sales for you and even hire people to do the coaching. Now, you have a business engine that can finance your dreams, finance your church's building project, and help countless missionaries and ministries fulfill their purpose.

Once I learned this concept, it changed my entire perspective on business. In my first year, I had made more money than I ever made in my life, all while continuing my mission work. I was 30 years old and had finally made six figures in a single year. However, the journey was not easy. It took a lot of work to dig myself out of the hole that I was in. Although I wasn't running that business full-time, it still enabled me to finance mission trips, give more to the ministries that I cared about, and travel the world, fulfilling my calling.

FAILURE IS A GIFT

Failure was my launchpad into my first true success in business. This experience taught me not to be discouraged if I didn't hit my business goals on my first try, second try, third try, and so forth. Each failure was a foundation for the next step of my journey.

As I reflect on my entrepreneurial history, there were many failures and mediocre business opportunities:

- Sold polished rocks at 8
- Started a vending machine business at 14
- Started a T-shirt company at 16
- Sold Prepaid Legal (now LegalShield) at 18
- Donated plasma at 19 (This counts! It paid my rent!)
- Sold glow sticks at music festivals at 21
- Became a donor-backed missionary at 22 and had to raise support
- Opened a digital marketing dealership at 27
- Recruited speakers at 28
- Started my digital marketing agency at 30

As you can see, it took ten businesses for me to finally be successful. It was actually more than that, but the others were so insignificant that they didn't justify a place on this list. I am sharing this for you to understand that regardless of where you are on your journey, it's never too late to start again. Don't be discouraged by past failures. The experience you gained during those seasons will be a crucial foundation for future seasons.

Here are a few examples of this from my life: starting a t-shirt company at 16 years old positioned me to tour rock festivals at 21. Touring rock festivals positioned me to meet my top donors and even led to some of the endorsements on this book! When I started selling Prepaid Legal at 18 years old, I was taught the value of personal development and learned extensive one-on-one sales strategies. This vital training was the foundation that helped me to have success in leading outreach tables on college campuses and teaching others how to talk to strangers. When I started selling digital marketing for my friend's company, it laid a foundation of knowledge through courses and experiences that would position me to eventually start my own digital marketing agency.

It was my knowledge in digital marketing that would enable me to launch an online Bible study with a friend that attracted over 1,000 registrants in just three days. If we keep having these Bible studies, I think that would qualify us as an online mega-church!

My business success enabled me to help finance many trips to Haiti and Vietnam. I took six trips to Vietnam in 2019 to do ministry. I would have never been able to do that if I didn't have a business that could help finance expensive flights around the world and hotel stays as we ministered there. On my first trip to Vietnam alone, our mission team did 17 church services in just 11 days. I had missionary friends who wanted to come and help with the impact we were making in Vietnam but couldn't afford to go on as many trips as I did.

DON'T BE DISCOURAGED BY PAST FAILURES. THE EXPERIENCE YOU GAINED DURING THOSE SEASONS WILL BE A CRUCIAL FOUNDATION FOR FUTURE SEASONS.

After a few years of playing "absentee entrepreneur," as I traveled the world doing missions alongside running a marketing agency, I even won the coveted 2 Comma Club award—which means I grossed $1,000,000 online using a prominent online software to capture prospective client contact information. Eventually, I was invited to join the Forbes Agency Council, an invitation-only community for senior-level agency executives which allows me to publish marketing articles on Forbes.com. As of this writing, the Forbes Agency Council even has me featured on their homepage.

What excites me the most besides writing this book is that I was granted a trademark for the word *LeadFlows*. I acquired the domain name LeadFlows.com and am building an exciting software brand around it.

When I first started my business, it was highly technical to build out a new patient system for chiropractors. I had to purchase landing page software, a two-way texting system, a tool for call tracking, a dedicated number for outbound calls, software for emails, software for online scheduling, software to send automated voicemails, and other systems. LeadFlows is an all-in-one sales and marketing platform that consolidates everything that I needed to individually purchase into a single solution. Every business, church, and non-profit will benefit from signing up for the software at LeadFlows.com.

As a thank you for following me on my journey, I have created a free online course you can get at WildExpectance.com/Start-Living that will inspire you to live your dream and even provide practical ways for you to finance your dreams too.

CHAPTER 22

WILD REFLECTANCE

I never wanted to be a missionary. It was my desire to make a lot of money and fund the Gospel. Yet, God knew me better than I knew myself. It turned out that I didn't have to make a lot of money to fund the Gospel; I didn't have to be a successful entrepreneur or even have a good job to be generous; I could do it all as a normal Christian. Better yet, I could fund the Gospel as a missionary myself. There were many times God would compel me to help others in need even when I didn't feel I could help myself.

Maybe I would be better at funding the Gospel if I understood the battles, the struggles, and the pain many missionaries face. The fear of being labeled a "beggar." The rejection of unmet expectations from family members. The constant looming feeling of inadequacy as I compared myself to my peers who had successful businesses or jobs, were married with children, and were living what seemed to be a perfect and worry-free life on social media.

Maybe God saved me from becoming one of those people, someone consumed only with themselves and their desires. Sure, I said I wanted to fund the Gospel, but did I really? Would I have had the boldness and confidence to be as generous as I am now if I hadn't lived it firsthand? As I reflect on my missionary journey, I believe God took me down this path because he wanted me to learn the difficulty.

For example, I've heard you tip better if you've worked in a restaurant as a waiter or a waitress. Maybe that's how it works with missions too. Maybe living as a missionary makes you more generous. Not only with your money, but with your time and attitude. I'm not saying that you need to leave your career and go live in an African hut to become generous, but maybe taking a mission trip somewhere will change you. If you decide to do this, I encourage you to choose someplace difficult. For example, you can't shake the change you experience coming back from a place like Haiti. In regards to that change, Haiti doesn't need you—you need Haiti.

When I started my business, I discovered that it was easier to get a chiropractor to pay my company thousands of dollars a month than to get a business person to support my mission work for hundreds a month. It was easier to get a successful chiropractor to direct deposit $55,000 into my company account than it was to get a successful business person to deposit $5,500 into our Haiti missions account. That much-needed $55,000 came right after I had just gotten back from one of my many trips to Vietnam. I took seven mission trips abroad that year and spent nearly 25% of the year as a missionary in Southeast Asia. As I mentioned in the previous chapter, I couldn't have afforded all of this if I didn't have a successful business. I may have been able to fundraise for one or two trips, but certainly not six transatlantic flights in addition to a flight to Haiti.

When I became a missionary, I learned that hearing from God wasn't as difficult as I thought. As a child, I would look to the pastor or guest speaker and imagine them as having this special line to God, reserved only for the "super Christians." That the person on stage was somehow "better" than me and heard from God in a special way that I never could. Worse yet, I thought deep intimacy with God was only achievable through 40-day fasts, mixed with a strict commitment to PG movies and Christian music. Though fasting and refraining from toxic shows are good, deep intimacy with God is achievable for all of us, wherever we are on our faith journey.

It's about making the conscious decision today that you want to know God in a deeper way. This choice will produce changes in your lifestyle, not the other way around. Now I know that normal, everyday people can hear from God regarding their life. God wants to use the *ordinary* to do the *extraordinary*. God wants to use you this way, but will you put in the extra effort of faith and action necessary?

A COMMITMENT TO THE CAUSE

I made sure I never misappropriated my "mission funds. " What I mean by that is when I finally achieved what many in the world deemed "success," I had problems spending my hard-earned money on whatever I wanted. I still felt like I was being held accountable, not to the donor or mission board this time, but to God, who was the source of my business success.

As the CEO of my business, I can spend my hard-earned money whichever way I please. However, I've seen too much, and I'm more interested in investing my hard-earned money into ministry than into an extravagant lifestyle. I've always gotten joy from generosity and experiences, not things. Do you know what's cooler than a Lamborghini or Bugatti? Feeding a hungry village in Haiti and sending impoverished kids to school. Do you know what's better than a yacht? Supporting missionaries around the world to fulfill their God-given purpose.

I STILL FELT LIKE I WAS BEING HELD ACCOUNTABLE, NOT TO THE DONOR OR MISSION BOARD THIS TIME, BUT TO GOD, WHO WAS THE SOURCE OF MY BUSINESS SUCCESS.

When I became a missionary, I thought it would have been close friends, family members, and my charismatic home church who would believe in me enough to support my mission work. Instead, most of my support came from an amazing Baptist couple from Texas I was introduced to one weekend at Lifest, a Christian music festival in Wisconsin. I will forever be grateful for them and how they believed in me in ways no one else had. It was this couple who bought me my Los Angeles vehicle. It was this couple who invested the most into my mission work in Haiti. It was this couple's monthly support that kept me on the front lines at UCLA. It was this couple who believed in me then and still believe in me now. I wouldn't have made it if it wasn't for their generosity during those tough years.

I want to be more like them and live their style of generosity. They give because God says to give, not because they expect anything in return. They are generous because they love the idea of seeing the younger generation, especially those on the college campuses, coming to know the Lord. They give because helping others brings them joy.

A DOUBLE MEANING

As I thought about how I was to end this book and this last chapter, I imagined I would conclude it with reflection. I thought it would be fun to have a pun on the name of the book and title it *"Wild Reflectance."* Was that even a word? I didn't know, but it sounded cool.

AS OTHER PEOPLE WATCH YOU AND ARE INSPIRED BY YOUR *WILD EXPECTANCE*, IT WILL CHALLENGE THEM TO STEP INTO THEIR CALLING.

As I looked up the word *reflectance*, I learned that it was a scientific term. Maybe it was something learned in physics class. I don't know because the closest I ever had to a physics class was when I road-tripped across the country with my German friend, the physics professor. Even then, I didn't learn about reflectance.

The Online Oxford Learners dictionary defines reflectance as "a measure of how much light is reflected off a surface, considered as a part of the total light that shines onto it."

When I thought about the definition, I realized that my final chapter had a double meaning. I encourage you to reflect on the stories I've shared and how to apply the principles I've learned in your own life. Reflect on and imagine the amazing God opportunities that await your future. Reflect on how you can hear from God for yourself, be more generous than you've ever been, and use your faith to do the impossible.

As you reflect on what you've learned from this book, what is the "measure of how much light is reflected off" of you and onto others? In other words, how is the message of this book not only deeply changing you but those around you? How does the message of this book compare to everything else (whether good or bad) that you're letting in through reading, television, video games, or however else you're spending your time?

There are different ways you can impact those around you: you can buy them a copy of this book, or you can sit down for coffee with a friend or family member and share with them some of the fun stories you've read.

I can imagine you doing this now: "Let me tell you this crazy story of a broke missionary who got a ride home from MC Hammer after he closed out the AMAs," or "I read about a guy who had the audacity to secretly give the college graduation check he received from his Jewish uncle to the church. Talk about awkward."

But maybe it's even more than that. Maybe it's sitting down with a friend and saying, "I think God is calling me to be a missionary. I know it doesn't make sense, and I don't have any money. But this guy, Bryan, did it, and it seemed to work out for him. Maybe I can do it, too."

Or, maybe God is calling you to finally pursue your passion, go on that much-needed vacation you always wanted, or even start a business.

I remember watching a show recently called *Undercover Billionaire*. They took a billionaire, dropped him off during the winter in a random city in Pennsylvania, and gave him $100, a beat-up truck, and a cell phone with limited data. He then had 90 days to build a business independently valued at $1 million dollars, or he had to invest $1 million of his own money into it.

People were so inspired by what he did that the next season, three more billionaires said they wanted to try this too. Maybe stepping out is you being that first billionaire. And as other people watch you and are inspired by your *wild expectance*, it will challenge them to step into their calling. Whatever you do, do it with the intent that generosity will always follow you.

Regardless of what amazing adventures your future holds, I would love to hear how this book has touched your life. Please visit WildExpectance.com/Story and share how this book has helped you in your spiritual journey. If you take a moment to submit your experience, I will send you some free bonus content that goes along with this book that you've not yet received.

I look forward to reading your story soon.

NEXT STEPS

1. Share how this book has touched your life at **WildExpectance.com/Story**.

2. Leave a review online on Amazon or Goodreads. For convenience purposes, you can use all or part of what you shared with us at the link above. Alternatively, you could leave a review of what you liked best about this book.

3. Get the scriptures referenced in this book as well as additional verses on the Holy Spirit at **WildExpectance.com/Scripture**.

4. If you work with a business, church, ministry, or non-profit, be sure to save money by consolidating your software and leveraging the top marketing automation system at **LeadFlows.com**.

5. If you are in business or are inspired to start a business, get my free course at **WildExpectance.com/Start-Living** to learn how to start making money online and even how to take your existing business to the next level so you can fulfill your God-given purpose.

6. Make a list of five people this book will help and surprise them with *Wild Expectance* as a gift.

7. Consider having Bryan speak at your church, conference, or event by filling out the form at **WildExpectance.com/Invite**.

8. Apply what you learned, embrace a life of *wild expectance*, and start living your life how God designed it.

REFERENCES

American Music Awards. "PSY & MC Hammer Gangnam Style." Filmed November 2012 at Nokia Theater L.A. Live, Los Angeles, CA. https://www.youtube.com/watch?v=5vUVPv0uPJs.

Assemblies of God. "Refugee Becomes Ministry Pioneer." Accessed April 7, 2022. https://news.ag.org/News/Refugee-Becomes-Ministry-Pioneer.

Cable News Network LP, LLLP. "Evolution debate: Student leads textbook challenge." Accessed April 12, 2022. http://www.cnn.com/2001/fyi/teachers.ednews/05/09/evolution.debate.

Cooke, Graham. Developing Your Prophetic Gifting. Lancaster: Sovereign World Ltd, 2000.

Chan, Francis. Crazy Love. Colorado Springs: David C. Cook, 2008.

Cunningham, Loren. Making Jesus Lord. Seattle: YWAM Publishing, 1988. Kindle.

Eastern District of Pennsylvania. "Joseph Baker and Maryn Teed v. Pennridge School District." Accessed April 12, 2022. https://www.paed.uscourts.gov/documents/opinions/03D0461P.pdf.

International House of Prayer. "Francis Chan Shares How He Connected With IHOP and Mike Bickle // IHOPKC // July 2021." Accessed April 7, 2022. https://www.youtube.com/watch?v=bNVY4djAUsM.

Jefferson University Hospitals. " Brazilian Mediums Shed Light on Brain Activity During a Trance State." Accessed April 7, 2022. https://hospitals. jefferson.edu/news/2012/11/brazilian-mediums-shed-light-on-brain-activity-during-a-trance-state.html.

McWilliams, Gail. Seeing Beyond: Choosing to Look Past the Horizon. Dallas: Brown Books Publishing Group, 2006.

Minnesota Public Radio. "Literary mysteries: The best-selling books of all time." Accessed April 9, 2022. https://www.mprnews.org/story/2015/07/21/thread-books-bcst-best-selling-books.

New York Times. "Haiti's President Assassinated in Nighttime Raid, Shaking a Fragile Nation." Accessed April 7, 2022. https://www.nytimes.com/2021/07/07/world/americas/haiti-president-assassinated-killed.html.

Nightline. "Speaking in Tongues Medical Study proves Holy Spirit praying." Accessed April 7, 2022. https://www.youtube.com/watch?v=NZbQBajYnEc.

O'Dell, Jerry and Marilyn O'Dell. The Wonderful, Powerful Gospel of Jesus Christ: Learn How to Share or Preach the Glorious Gospel of Power!. Pine Knot: O'Dell Ministries, 1999.

Ollison, Larry. Unlocking the Mysteries of the Holy Spirit. Shippensburg: Harrison House Publishers, 2016.

Oxford University Press. "Reflectance." Accessed April 12, 2022. https://www.oxfordlearnersdictionaries.com/us/definition/american_english/reflectance.

Regents of University of California. "UCLA ranked No. 13 in the world by U.S. News and World Report." Accessed 24 April 2017. https://newsroom.ucla.edu/releases/ucla-ranked-no-13-in-the-world-by-u-s-news-and-world-report.

Roberson, Dave. The Walk of the Spirit - The Walk of Power: The Vital Role of Praying in Tongues. Tulsa: Dave Roberson Ministries, 2012.

REFERENCES

Sithole, Surprise. *Voice in the Night: The True Story of a Man and the Miracles That Are Changing Africa.* Minnesota: Chosen Books, 2012.

The Gospel Coalition. "How Much Do You Have to Hate Somebody to Not Proselytize?" Accessed April 12, 2022. https://www.thegospelcoalition.org/blogs/justin-taylor/how-much-do-you-have-to-hate-somebody-to-not-proselytize.

U.S. Embassy. "Security Alert: Department of State's Travel Advisory for Haiti (July 9, 2018)." Accessed April 7, 2022. https://ht.usembassy.gov/security-alert-department-of-states-travel-advisory-for-haiti-july-9-2018.

Washington Post. "Southern Baptists to Open Their Ranks to Missionaries Who Speak in tongues." Accessed April 7, 2022. https://www.washingtonpost.com/national/religion/southern-baptists-to-open-their-ranks-to-missionaries-who-speak-in-tongues/2015/05/14/1fddd28a-fa7e-11e4-a47c-e56f4db884ed_story.html.

ACKNOWLEDGMENTS

I want to first thank the Lord for inspiring me to start writing down stories during a church service near Apple Valley, CA, and for leading me on this wild journey.

I want to thank Dr. Richard Nongard, who I sat by at a marketing conference and with whom I shared the importance of building a LeadFlow. It wasn't a coincidence that we met. Your initiative to schedule onto my calendar to talk about how to market your course eventually helped me accomplish something I dreamed of doing for years. You provided invaluable coaching, accountability, and the practical steps necessary that enabled me to focus and make this book a reality.

I want to also thank Winston Bui for believing in me. Your valuable mentorship over the years and the numerous ministry trips we have taken together across the United States and the world have been truly impactful. Without you, there wouldn't be much to write about in this book because you were the catalyst that launched me into missions.

I want to thank Sean Smith for your support and prophetic mentorship that has helped me hear from God more significantly.

I want to thank Joe Baker for all the wild adventures we've experienced together on the road that I get to write about in this book. We share so many incredible stories that I wanted to tell but didn't have the space to include.

Thank you, David, for being an amazing, supportive brother and a role model to look up to my entire life. You set a great example of how I should live and were the one who introduced me to Chi Alpha, which changed the trajectory of my entire life.

Thank you, Phil and Roberta Cuilty, for your continued leadership through your sensitivity to the Holy Spirit and for being there for me during my senior year in college.

Thank you, KC Wright, for your years of friendship and valuable insights into the radio world.

Thank you, Dr. Larry Ollison, for teaching me the foundation of faith at an early age that has followed me my entire life.

Thank you, Dr. Nasir Siddiki, for your vast knowledge of the word of God and practical teachings on generosity.

Thank you, Dr. Daniel King, for your inspiration in mass evangelism and crusade ministry around the world.

Thank you, Chi Alpha family, and all the incredible people I've met along the way and worked alongside in missions that have helped shape me into who I am today.

Thank you, Grandma, Miriam, and everyone else who has supported me, provided valuable feedback, and helped make this book the best.

Thank you to everyone who has believed in my ministry over the years, has been a prayer warrior on my behalf, and invested financially in my mission work. I want to thank the many other spiritual mentors, friends, and family members who have been there for me in my life.

Thank you Dr. Nathan Francis for your editorial help and the perspective you provided as I endeavored to finish this book. I'm forever grateful for the like-minded faith we share and our many adventures together while you were at UCLA.

Thank you to my hardworking editorial team at Raindrop Creative and Start Write, including Rainah Davis, Tiara Brown, Dr. Erin Almond, and Dr. Gerald C. Simmons.

Thank you Cara Lockwood and BK Wells for your final editorial review right before publication.

Thank you, Scott Spiewak, for believing in this book and providing crucial PR support.

ACKNOWLEDGMENTS

Thank you, Charity Reeb, for your creative inspiration and introduction to the fabulous team at Printopya and NEWTYPE Publishing.

Thank you, Ryan Sprenger and Abigail Taylor, for helping me navigate distribution channels and printing schedules.

And last but not least, thank you Chelsea for responding to my text for help with this book. I never imagined your "YES" to agreeing to help me would result in us falling in love.

ABOUT THE AUTHOR

Bryan Citrin is an in-demand public speaker and entrepreneur driven by a heart for people. He was forever impacted by his first mission trip to Haiti. There, he was broken by the drastic needs of families living in dirt floor huts and children going hungry. He met people without an opportunity for an education or work.

Bryan launched an online marketing business to financially help the many needs he saw. His company quickly took off, enabling him to help business leaders around the United States.

He has now traveled for mission work all over the world, including six trips to Vietnam and 28 trips to Haiti. In the United States, he has mentored students through a campus ministry for over a decade at universities such as the University of California, Los Angeles (UCLA) and the University of Southern California (USC).

Bryan has a Bachelor of Science in Entrepreneurship, is a Two Comma Club Award winner, and is an active member of the Forbes Agency Council.

In his free time, Bryan loves adventure sports like snowboarding, rock climbing, and sleeping on a portaledge off the side of cliffs.